Kelly J. Haack

Family Faith Walks

On-the-Go Faith Activities

CONCORDIA PUBLISHING HOUSE • SAINT LOUIS

To Jim, my encourager, sounding board, and dear husband.

And to Caleb and Christian, may you always love Jesus and walk in the faith.

Scripture quotations are taken from the Holy Bible, New International Version® NIV®. Copyright © 1973, 1978, 1984 by International Bible Society. Used by permission of Zondervan Publishing House. All rights reserved.

Portions of this book are excerpted from: *Luther's Small Catechism with Explanation* © 1986 Concordia Publishing House. All rights reserved.

Text copyright © 2002 Kelly J. Haack

Illustrations copyright © 2002 Concordia Publishing House
Cover design by Jennifer Horton-Beck
Illustrations by Michelle Dorenkamp

Published by Concordia Publishing House
3558 S. Jefferson Avenue, St. Louis, MO 63118-3968

Manufactured in the United States of America

Library of Congress Cataloging-in-Publication Data

Haack, Kelly J., 1967-
   Family faith walks : on-the-go faith activities / Kelly J. Haack.
      p. cm.
  ISBN 0-7586-0045-3
 1. Family--Prayer-books and devotions--English. 2.
Children--Prayer-books and devotions--English. I. Title.
  BV255 .H22 2002
  249-dc21

1   2   3   4   5   6   7   8   9   10   11   10   09   08   07   06   05   04   03   02

Contents

APRIL

MAY

JUNE

JULY

AUGUST

SEPTEMBER

OCTOBER

NOVEMBER

DECEMBER

THROUGH THE YEAR

Appendix A:

Appendix B:

Introduction

Children in Action

What are some of your child's favorite activities? Sports? Birthday parties? Visiting amusement parks? Splashing in a pool?

If your child is like most children, it is the *active* in *activities* that brings a smile to his face and puts a bounce in his step. Children love to move. They love to do. Children love to live life to the fullest.

Children in action. It is upon this concept that *Family Faith Walks: On-the-Go Faith Activities* was written. An old proverb states, "Tell me and I forget, show me and I remember, involve me and I understand." Our hope as parents is that our children will not only grow in their faith in Christ, but that they will celebrate it as much as they celebrate life.

Children in action. *Family Faith Walks* uses walks through the neighborhood, hikes in parks, games, crafts, and a multitude of other creative activities in conjunction with God's Word, prayers, and discussion starters to help children understand, celebrate, and live their faith to the fullest.

Active Learning and More

Family Faith Walks was designed not only to be a devotional resource bursting with active learning ideas to help you, the parent, nurture your child in her faith, but to be a valuable resource in a variety of ways.

Flexibility. Because each family is unique, one-size-does-not-fit-all when it comes to devotions. With a multitude of devotional topics, activities, and styles, *Family Faith Walks* offers flexibility. Feel free to choose and adapt the ideas that best fit your family. As you do, keep in mind that family devotions serve as an extension of the worship your family experiences within your community of faith. Adapt your devotional needs according to your family's worship needs.

Equipping the parent. God has given you the significant vocation of passing on your faith as a heritage to your children (see the words of Moses in

Deuteronomy 6:4–9). But for you to be properly equipped, it is important for you to grow in your own faith walk. In each devotion, a section titled *Ponderings* is dedicated to helping you, the parent, dig deeper into the Word of God so you might be equipped to be a spiritual mentor for your children.

Faith communication. Family faith communication is key to nurturing the growing faith of children. *Family Faith Walks* provides discussion questions, models of where and when to initiate faith talk, and meditations to help you grow in your faith and understanding of God's Word and better communicate your faith to your children.

Faith in Life. These devotions are brimming with opportunities to reinforce what God's Word teaches us about how our heavenly Father is active and connected to everyday life. A walk in the wind is a reminder of the power of the Holy Spirit. A Valentine card is a witness to God's love. And a snack of "Cloud Puffs" is a yummy object lesson that reinforces the story of Christ's ascension. Soon your child will see God in every part of life!

Getting Started

Family Faith Walks was written to help you in your role as a faith mentor to your children as you are drawn closer to God in your own personal faith. I strongly urge you to pray that the Holy Spirit will lead your words and actions. Read and study the Scripture for the week, *God's Grace to Us*, and the section called *Faith Talk*. Use the section titled *Ponderings* to delve deeper into Scripture. Five devotional thoughts are included, one for each weekday. Go through these devotional thoughts the week before leading your children through a particular devotion or during the same week. As you do so, God will fill you with His grace, equipping you to pass on the heritage of faith in Christ to your children.

Using this Book

These devotions are designed to help you weave God into your daily, busy lives. Read the descriptions for each section, then decide how they can be woven into your days and weeks.

God's Grace to Us

The Scripture lesson provided in this section establishes the spiritual focus for the week. I recommend that you share with your children the complete text from the Bible, since many of the devotional thoughts and activities refer to the larger Scripture reading. Memorizing the particular passage listed is a wonderful way to write God's Word upon the hearts of your children. Rather than simply learning to recite the passages, incorporate them into various activities throughout the week. Remember, God's Word is at the heart of our devotional lives.

Faith Walk

The faith walks have been designed to offer quality time with your children so God's world around you can be used as a connection to His Word and a means for you to communicate and demonstrate your faith. Many of the thoughts introduced in Faith Talk can be easily discussed during the walk.

Faith Talk

The discussion points provided are to be used as a springboard or launching pad for discussion. They will help you help your children expand upon God's Word. The points can be easily discussed during the walk, during devotional times at your home altar, or in the course of other family activities, such as during carpool or mealtimes. Take time to read and meditate on these thoughts prior to sharing them with your children. If you want further insight into a question or faith topic, ask your pastor to lead you to helpful resources. Please note that they can be used either word for word or adapted as best fit your needs.

Follow-up Activities

Games, craft projects, simple recipes, and other fun activities in this section reinforce the spiritual emphasis for the week. They put the focus into practice and add an element of excitement to the devotions. Feel free to use the activities that work best for your family.

Our Response to God's Grace

The prayers offered help your family focus on the spiritual emphasis as they approach God in response to His gifts of grace. You can use them as written or make them your own, changing and adding to them as they touch your family's heart. Keep in mind that you and your children will also benefit from traditional prayers such as the Lord's Prayer and Luther's morning and evening prayers. Feel free to use these favorites as well.

Ponderings

Scripture, prayer, meditation, journaling, and a variety of other activities are woven into these devotions designed for you, the parent. I recommend that you study and meditate on only one point each day so you can give it adequate attention, helping it become part of your spiritual fabric.

God draws you closer to Him through His Word, thereby strengthening you to share your own spiritual heritage with your family and to pass along the inheritance you share as heirs of His kingdom. Set time aside for these weekly devotions, just as you dedicate time each week to join with others in your family of faith for worship as God comes to you through His means of His grace—His Word and the sacraments of Holy Communion and Baptism.

Journal Jottings

Make this book your family's own. Space is provided at the end of each devotion for you to record your reflections on the Ponderings section, chronicle your family's faith journey, or recall comments or questions that arise during your walk or faith discussion. You may also use this space to paste a photo of your family's activities or to note other ways you and your children recognize or celebrate our heavenly Father's presence and power in your lives.

Creating a Home Altar

Throughout this book, you will see reference to a home altar. Set aside a special place where your family comes together on a regular basis to pray, praise, and grow together in God's grace.

Some ideas for a family altar include:

✧ A coffee table with a cross on top of it

✧ Candles on the dinner table

✧ A shelf with a beautiful Bible prominently displayed

✧ A low table draped with a decorative cloth and adorned with a picture of Jesus

✧ A combination of the above, or any other spot in your home where your family's focus can be directed away from daily cares onto God and His love for us through Christ

In addition, find a place for keeping a Bible, devotion books, and other worship materials where they are easily accessible.

*It is my hope that **Family Faith Walks** is a vehicle for God's Spirit to work through you to your children, as together you walk the road of faith.*

Kelly J. Haack

January

New Year's Blessings

God's Grace to Us

Today's Reading: Psalm 103

For as high as the heavens are above the earth, so great is His love for those who fear Him. Psalm 103:11

Faith Walk

Walk through your home, your yard, and your neighborhood. Look for ways the Lord has blessed you (e.g., a place to call home, a pet to love, neighbors who help, etc.).

Faith Talk

✧ Reflect on the past year. How has God blessed you?

✧ Why does God bless you? Reread the Bible passage.

✧ Reread Psalm 103. Make a list of the many ways God blesses us.

✧ What is our response to God's blessings?

✧ How can we be a blessing from God to others?

Follow-up Activities

✤ On a large white tablecloth, use fabric markers to draw and write the blessings God has given you. Use this tablecloth periodically throughout the year ahead.

✤ Cover and decorate a shoebox. Label it "Blessing Box." In the months ahead, drop a coin in the box each time you take note of how God has blessed your family or someone in your family. At the end of the year, donate the money to a missionary your congregation supports or to an organization that serves the needy.

✤ Look through photos from the past year and talk about the many blessings each one represents.

✤ Be a blessing to God's creation. Scatter birdseed, breadcrumbs, and bits of fruits and vegetables outside for the birds and squirrels.

✤ Write a family psalm recalling God's blessings. Use it as a prayer before meals or at bedtime.

Our Response to God's Grace

Dear Loving Father,

You have blessed me with many gifts. For this I praise and thank You. Most of all, I thank You for the blessing of sending Jesus as my Savior. Help me to be a blessing to others. In the name of Jesus, my Gift. Amen.

Ponderings

☞ God has blessed us with His Word, a 66-book love letter, from which we can drink daily of His love poured out for us. Every word, phrase, and verse is God inviting us to see, hear, taste, touch, and feel His love. It is God comforting, encouraging, strengthening, blessing, and inspiring. It is a picture of God: loving, righteous, all-powerful (omnipotent), all-present (omnipresent), all-knowing (omniscient), the "I AM" (see Exodus 3:14). Drink of God's Word daily.

☞ God blesses us with the blood of His Son, Jesus, poured out for us. Blood donors are said to have given "the gift of life." Jesus gave His life, sacrificed on the cross, and His death, through which our sins were nailed to the cross so we might receive "the gift of eternal life." Eat of His body and drink of His blood at the Lord's Table and receive the rich blessing of forgiveness poured out for you.

∽ God blesses us with the forgiveness bought for us with Christ's life, death, and resurrection. The stains of our sins are washed away by Christ's blood. We are free of the burden of guilt and God's righteous anger and punishment as deserved because of our sins. Christ carried the burden of guilt for us. We are free! Repent and drink of the freedom of forgiveness.

∽ God blesses us with His life-giving Spirit, poured out on us through the waters of Baptism and producing in us the fruit of faith. Faith multiplies God's blessings. Through faith in Christ, we receive salvation, hope, and comfort. Faith enables us to do God's will and gives meaning and purpose to our lives. Drink from the water of life—God's Spirit—and be rich in faith.

∽ God blesses us by restoring our relationship with Him. Sin separates us from God Himself. It also breaks apart the intimacy of our earthly relationships, but God soothes our lonely spirits and pain-filled hearts as we cry out. Through Christ and His death, all barriers are broken. Our souls, yearning for intimacy, unconditional love, and wholeness, find them in our Lord. Approach Him in prayer. Seek Him in worship. Drink of your relationship with God through His Word and His love poured out for you through the body and blood of Christ.

Journal Jottings

In the Beginning

God's Grace to Us

Today's Reading: Genesis 1:1–2:3

In the beginning God created the heavens and the earth. Genesis 1:1

Faith Walk

Take a walk to a park. 1. Look at the heavens and the earth. Describe what you see. 2. Close your eyes and imagine nothingness. Describe what "nothingness" looks like. 3. Imagine summer. Describe what summer looks like. Now compare the three pictures and imagine God creating the world. As you walk, see if you can name the order in which God created the whole world.

Faith Talk

✧ It is a New Year, a new beginning. The first New Year was "in the beginning [when] God created the heavens and the earth."

✧ What does it mean to create?

✧ Discuss the magnitude of God's power in that He created the whole universe from nothing, using only His words.

✧ Compare God's ability to create with our ability to create.

✧ God created everything. All we can do is change things to make them seem new. As the creator of everything, God is also the owner of everything. Out of love He lets us receive the blessings of His creation. In return, how should we treat God's creation?

Follow-up Activities

🍁 Reread the entire passage for this week. Review the days of creation. Draw pictures for each day.

🍁 Make people shapes from play dough or clay. (See Appendix B for a homemade play dough recipe.) Are you able to breathe the breath of life into your people shapes like God did to Adam?

🍁 God created you. Write a list of ways you can take care of the body God gave you.

🍁 Keep a chronicle of a year in God's creation:

1. Each month take one or two pictures of your yard or a special place in a park.

2. Mount the pictures on a sheet of paper. Label them with the date the pictures were taken.

3. Punch three evenly spaced holes on the left side of each piece of paper.

4. Bind the papers together with ribbon or yarn to make a simple photo album. Write a caption for each picture.

5. Look through the book of Psalms for a Bible verse that reflects the praise you feel when you see God's creation. Write the verse you chose on the very last page of your book.

🍁 Be wise stewards of God's creation. Make a plan to reduce waste in your home by throwing away less food, turning off lights more frequently, or recycling more materials. Give any money you save back to God.

Our Response to God's Grace

Dear Creator God,

You created the heavens and the earth, everything in them, and me. I own nothing. All of creation is Yours. And in Your love, You have blessed me with the gifts of Your creation. In return, please help me to use these gifts wisely by taking care of Your creation and giving a portion back to You through my offerings of time and money. By the power of Jesus' name. Amen.

Ponderings

↝ "In the beginning ..." As you begin a New Year, ponder how you treat God's creation. What kind of a relationship do you have? What, through the power of Christ, can you do to improve how you relate to God's creation and bring glory to Him?

↝ It is often a temptation to place God's creation above God Himself, the Creator. In what ways might this happen? How can we, in turn, put God above creation?

↝ What can you do to honor God through His creation?

↝ As the Creator of all, God is the owner of everything who richly blesses us with the gifts of His creation. Take time to examine your attitudes. Have you, perhaps, fallen into the trap of believing you are the owner of everything? Or do you see yourself as being entrusted with the care of God's creation? Which attitude do you feel describes how you feel? How does this attitude affect what you do?

↝ Read some additional passages on God's creation and praise God for His marvelous gifts: Psalm 148, Ezekiel 34:25–31, and 1 Timothy 4:4–5.

Journal Jottings

Following the Star

God's Grace to Us

Today's Reading: Matthew 2:1–12

"Where is the one who has been born King of the Jews? We saw His star in the east and have come to worship Him." Matthew 2:2

Faith Walk

Take a walk on a clear night. Look for the brightest star in the sky. When you find it, retell the story of the Wise Men coming to worship Christ, the King.

Faith Talk

✧ Close your eyes and imagine being one of the Wise Men following the star night after night. It took a long time to reach Bethlehem. What do you think they talked about as they traveled?

✧ How do you think the Wise Men felt to have finally found the Christ Child? Reread Matthew 2:10–11. What do these words tell us happened?

✧ Jesus, the King of the Jews, was revealed (shown) to the Wise Men through God's Word and the star. That's how they found out who Jesus was. How do *you* know about Jesus?

✧ Why did Jesus become a baby and come to earth?

✧ The Bible tells us that the Wise Men worshiped Jesus. How can *we* worship Jesus?

Follow-up Activities

❧ Hide a doll or stuffed animal. Have one person lead the family around the house to look for it. After finding it, form a circle holding hands and sing a Christmas song of worship.

❧ Make and decorate cookies shaped like stars.

❧ God Himself has come to earth as Jesus! Alleluia! How many ways can you think of to offer your praise and thanksgiving to Jesus? Choose one idea and carry it out.

❧ Give Jesus a gift to show Him your love. For example, visit an elderly relative or neighbor, give a gift of time or food to a homeless shelter, or read a book to a younger child. Let the love of Christ shine through you to others.

❧ Write thank-you notes for the Christmas gifts you received. Then thank God for the gift of His Son.

Our Response to God's Grace

Dear God, our Father,

You revealed Jesus to us at our Baptism and through Your Word. Help us to continue to grow in knowledge and faith as we study Your Word. Help us to lead others to You by telling them the story of Jesus and His love. In His name. Amen.

Ponderings

✍ Epiphany is the season in which we recall the many ways Jesus was revealed to us as the Savior. Reflect on the meaning of Christ the Savior in your life.

✍ Read these additional Epiphany stories:
Matthew 3:13–17
Matthew 4:1–11
Luke 2:21–40
John 2:1–11

✍ What was revealed about Christ in each of these stories?

✍ How does Christ reveal Himself to you?

✍ How can you reflect the love of Christ and lead others to God's revelations in Word and Sacrament?

✍ The Wise Men presented three gifts to the Christ Child. Each gift prophesied who Jesus truly was. The gold was the gift of a king for the King of the Jews and of all who believe. Priests burned incense when bringing their petitions (requests), before God. Jesus, the true High Priest, is the Mediator between God and us. Myrrh, an oil, was applied to a body at a person's burial. This gift prophesied Christ crucified. Based on these roles of Jesus, what kind of a relationship can we have with Him?

Journal Jottings

A New Creation

God's Grace to Us

Today's Reading: 2 Corinthians 5:11–21

Therefore, if anyone is in Christ, he is a new creation; the old has gone, the new has come! 2 Corinthians 5:17

Faith Walk

Take a two-part walk. For the first half of the walk, look for all the ways the world seems to be asleep for the winter—bare tree branches, brown grass, shorter and darker days, fewer or no flowers. For the second half of the walk, look for signs of a new creation—newly formed snowflakes, evergreen trees, animal tracks, and birds. God has made you a new creation!

Faith Talk

✧ God the Creator continues to create and take care of His creation, even in the winter.

✧ Through God the Holy Spirit, He continues to create a new and clean heart within us.

✧ What is the old creation like? Read Romans 3:10–18.

✧ What is the new creation like? Read Ezekiel 36:25–30.

✧ What does God promise for those with a new and clean heart?
  Read Revelation 21:1–6.

Follow-up Activities

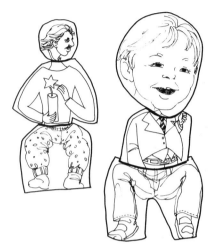

🍁 Create mixed-up people pictures:

   1. Cut pictures of people from magazines.

   2. Cut each picture into three parts: head, body, and legs. Mix up the parts and glue them onto paper so the head of one person is with the body of a second person and the legs of a third person.

   3. Like our pictures, we have been mixed up by sin. But Jesus has made us a new creation—forgiven and new.

🍁 Cut snowflakes from paper. Make each one different, just as real snowflakes are individually different. God's creativity is endless.

🍁 Color the tips of your thumbs with washable markers. Press onto paper to make thumbprints. Compare your prints with one another's. No two are alike. God's creativity is endless.

🍁 Have a "New Year—New Creation" party. If you live where it is cold, create snow or ice sculptures outside. Or make toothpick and marshmallow sculptures inside. Decorate and cut out hearts as a reminder that we are a new creation in Christ. Blow horns to celebrate God's creation of a New Year.

🍁 Write New Year's resolutions. As you do, ask, "How can I show others that I am a new creation in Christ?"

Our Response to God's Grace

Dear Creator God,

With the blood of Jesus, You have washed my sins away and made my heart clean. I am a new creation. Help me to live as Your child as I await Your final creation—new heavens and a new earth in eternal life. In the Savior's name I pray. Amen.

Ponderings

❧ Read 2 Corinthians 5:14–21. This passage explains what it means to be a new creation. Rephrase it using your own words. What implications does this verse have in your life?

❧ Christians are sinners; we cannot escape our sinful desires and often succumb to them. But Christians are at the same time saints; God has redeemed us through Christ by removing the guilt of our sin, and the Holy Spirit works faith in our hearts so we might live according to God's will. Paul knew this internal struggle well. Read about it in Romans 7:14–25. What is God's answer to this dilemma? Read Romans 8:1–4.

❧ What internal struggles do you experience? Confess them to God in prayer. Accept His healing balm of forgiveness. Ask God to help you change. Cling to the promise of a struggle-free eternal life.

❧ Sanctification is the continual process in which God's Spirit makes each of us a new creation. Through God's Word and the sacraments of Baptism and Holy Communion, God comes to us, making us a clearer image of Himself and enabling us to better reflect Him in our spirit and actions. But we are by nature sinful and unclean. Sometimes we stumble and backslide. At these times, we seek God's forgiveness through Jesus and His help in starting over. We are both sinner and saint. How would you describe God's sanctification in your life?

❧ In what ways could you be a better reflection of God's love to others? Make one or two New Year's resolutions to shine anew. Pray for God's Spirit to help you. When you fail, remember that you are a new creation, beautiful in the sight of the Lord. Repent, be forgiven, and start afresh!

Journal Jottings

Snow White

God's Grace to Us

Today's Reading: Psalm 51:1–12

Cleanse me with hyssop, and I will be clean; wash me, and I will be whiter than snow. Psalm 51:7

Faith Walk

If you live where the snow falls, take a walk on a snowy day. Examine the snowflakes as they fall on your hair, mittens, and clothes. Look for color contrasts—a white snowflake on a dark mitten or white snow piled on a brown branch. When our sins are forgiven, we are made whiter than snow.

Faith Talk

✧ What does the psalmist mean when he says, "... wash me, and I will be whiter than snow?"

✧ Have you ever been outside when the snow is so bright that it hurts your eyes to look at it? When our sins are forgiven, in God's eyes we are whiter, brighter, more pure and clean than even the brightest, most blinding snow.

✧ Imagine falling into a muddy creek, being sprayed by a skunk, or stumbling into an ants' nest. How would you feel? Would you feel better or worse after a bath? Now think about the dirtiness of sin and the cleansing bath of God's forgiveness. How does that make you feel?

✧ Verse 8a says, "Let me hear joy and gladness." What would you do if you or your favorite team won a sporting event? Would you cheer? Clap? Jump up and down? Do a dance or hug someone? After all, you have won a major event! When Christ died, you won forgiveness. The trophy is heaven. That's the best victory of all! It's worth cheering about!

✧ Next time you see new clean snow, give a cheer!

Follow-up Activities

❀ Hunt for white items in your home. Put them in a pile and say a prayer thanking God for making you whiter than all of them.

❀ Mix water and red food coloring in a spray bottle. Go outside and spray a heart in fresh snow. God has cleansed your heart from sin.

❀ Create a picture as a reminder that Jesus died on the cross to make our hearts clean from sin and white as snow:

1. Use a doily as a snowflake.

2. Cut out a heart and a cross. (See patterns in Appendix B.)

3. Glue the heart to the snowflake. Glue the cross on the heart.

4. Hang the pictures above your beds.

❀ Have a clown day. Use face paint to make white faces. Put a heart, cross, or other symbols of God's love on your face. Act out a favorite Bible story using no words.

❀ Get your hands filthy. Then wash them clean. As your hands are clean, so is your heart clean from the stain of sin through God's forgiveness.

Our Response to God's Grace

Dear Heavenly Father,

Thank You for washing my sins away and making my heart whiter than snow. With gladness and joy, I praise You for Your love to me. Alleluia! For the sake of Jesus, who shed His blood for me. Amen.

Ponderings

✐ Read Psalm 51:5. What genetic traits have been passed to you from previous generations? Unfortunately, some parents pass to their children genetic traits that result in psychological, physical, or mental disabilities. These problems may not show up at birth but they are inherent. In the same way, our first parents, Adam and Eve, passed on to us, not a genetic problem, but a nature of sin. How does knowing this affect your answer to this question: How can an "innocent" infant be sinful?

✐ If we are sinful by nature, can a cosmetic change "fix" the problem? No! We cannot fix the problem by attempting to change our behavior. Our very nature needs to be changed. Read Romans 6:1–4 to find out how this is done. For a better understanding, read Romans 5:12–21.

✐ How does our new nature change us? Read Romans 6:15–23.

✐ How are you changed by your new nature?

✐ Every day, for one week, read Romans chapters five and six. Write a response to what you have read.

Journal Jottings

Winter Fun

God's Grace to Us

Today's Reading: Ecclesiastes 3:1–8

[There is] ... a time to laugh. Ecclesiastes 3:4b

Faith Walk

Take a "winter fun walk" and look for ways to be silly and create laughter. If you live in a place where there is snow, stomp through the highest snow piles you can find. Roll down a hill. Throw snow in the air and twirl around as it lands on your head. Have fun and laugh! Thank God for giving you a time to laugh.

Faith Talk

✧ What other ways can you have "winter fun"?

✧ Why is laughter good for a person? A family?

✧ Read all eight verses of the Bible selection. What are some of the "times" you have in your family life?

✧ Remember some of the happy, sad, difficult, and warm times your family has had. What are your favorite family times? Thank Jesus for the happy times and for His help during difficult times.

✧ How can you use your time to glorify God?

Follow-up Activities

❧ Plan a winter fun outing. Some suggested activities: sledding, ice skating, skiing, making snow sculptures, or having a snowball fight.

❧ Make a list of "family fun" activities you would like to do in the upcoming year.

✤ Plan a time to do something, as a family, to help someone in need. For example, call your church for the name of a shut-in who needs a ride to get a haircut or to buy groceries. Offer to help.

✤ Plan a time to do something, as a family, for your church. For example, offer to clean a neglected corner of God's house.

✤ Have a family meeting to evaluate how you use your time. Are you over-involved in extra activities? Are you neglecting areas of your life that are important? Do you place a priority on making time to attend worship as a family? Does everyone have time to work and relax, be alone and with one another and friends? Based on your evaluation, adjust your schedules and commitments or keep them the same.

Our Response to God's Grace

Dear Father in Heaven,

You are the creator of all time. Thank You for the gift of time, for both good times and difficult times. Teach us to use our time wisely. For Jesus' sake. Amen.

Ponderings

✐ Reread the Scripture selection. Discerning how to best use and balance time can be a constant struggle. Ask for God's wisdom and guidance in this task and for forgiveness when you fail.

✐ Keep a journal of how you use your time and, after a month, evaluate where your time goes.

✐ Make schedule changes accordingly. If this is a consistent problem, seek the guidance of a trusted friend or counselor.

✐ Do you include God as part of all of the times of your life? As sinners, this is an impossible task. In Matthew 28:20b, Jesus says, "And surely I am with you always, to the very end of the age." When we fail to make God a part of our lives, Christ is by our sides forgiving us. He is also there to help us strive to make this most important change in our lives.

꙯ God has blessed us with the gift of time. He loves us and wants us to have time for rest and spiritual renewal. That is why He created the Sabbath. Do you honor the Sabbath times in your life? First and foremost, we honor the Sabbath by attending regular worship so we might be renewed by His saving grace. But Sabbath times can also be an early-morning prayer time; a day spent alone when the children are with another trusted adult; or a solitary walk. Make a date to be alone with God, reflect on His Word, and receive His refreshing love!

꙯ Read Proverbs 16:1–9. Who is in control of our times? How can that shape our attitudes and practices?

Journal Jottings

February

Lay Down Your Life Love

Gift of Government

Lamb of God

Windy Weather

Love in Action

Take up the Cross

Lay Down Your Life Love

God's Grace to Us

Today's Reading: John 15:9–17

"Greater love has no one than this, that He lay down his life for his friends." John 15:13

Faith Walk

Take a walk through a mall or other shopping area. Point out signs, pictures, and other reminders of St. Valentine's Day. What is love?

Faith Talk

✧ How do these Valentine's Day signs portray love? How do Christians demonstrate love?

✧ Read John 3:16. How has God shown His love for us?

✧ The world sees love as a feeling. Christians see love as an action. How are these two views of love different? What is meant by sacrificial love?

✧ St. Valentine was a Christian whose love for God and unsaved people was so great that he witnessed God's love to the point of being killed for his faith.

✧ How can you put your love for God and others into action?

Follow-up Activities

❧ Make St. Valentine's Day cards "from God" for friends and family. Write love messages as if God were writing them. Use Bible verses to help you. Some possible verses are the Scripture verses for this lesson, John 3:16, 1 John 4:7–21, 1 Corinthians 13:4–7, or Isaiah 54:10.

- Have a St. Valentine's Day party. Invite each guest to bring a gift of love: a can of food or other nonperishable item for a food pantry. Make St Valentine's Day cards and clay heart ornaments to take to a nursing home. (See page 282 in Appendix B for directions for making ornaments). For a snack, serve red punch and finger gelatin cut into heart shapes.

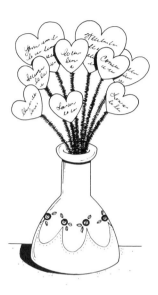

- Make a "love bouquet":

  1. Cut hearts from red construction paper. Make them several sizes and shapes.

  2. On each heart, write a way God shows His love for us.

  3. Tape the hearts to chenille wires. Arrange your "flowers" in a vase.

- Have each family member write a list of ways other people make them feel loved. Post the lists and make a commitment to show family members that they are loved.

- Research the history of St. Valentine's Day and make a book about it.

Our Response to God's Grace

Dear God, Loving Jesus,

Your love for us was so great that You suffered a painful and humiliating death on the cross so we might have life. We can love because You first loved us. Help us, in return, to reach out to others in love. In Your loving name we pray. Amen.

Ponderings

- Read Genesis 22:1–19 and Luke 22:41–44. Compare the heartache God the Father must have felt as He listened to His beloved Son crying out to Him in the garden to the heartache Abraham must have felt as he was about to sacrifice his beloved and long-awaited son. Now imagine yourself being asked to sacrifice your child or children. What can we learn from these stories about God's love for us and the love we are called to give back to Him?

- Read 1 Corinthians 13:4–7. Rewrite this passage as if God were describing His love for you personally. For example, the words "Love is patient, love is kind," could be rewritten as "When you use My name in vain, My love is patient. When you are in pain because you mistreated your body, My love is kind." Rewrite this passage a second time, describing your own love for your family.

- Read Song of Songs in the Old Testament. As you read this book of the Bible, look at it through two lenses. The first lens is that of two lovers. The second lens is that of God describing His love for you.

- God's love for you is an action. It is God crying when you cry, disciplining when you sin, calling when you stray, rejoicing when you return, and sacrificing Himself when you were lost. Keep a journal of God's love, documenting the many ways He reaches out to you in love each day.

- Spend quiet time in prayer, asking God to help you reach out to others in sacrificial love.

Journal Jottings

Gift of Government

God's Grace to Us

Today's Reading: Romans 13:1–7

Everyone must submit himself to the governing authorities, for there is no authority except that which God has established. The authorities that exist have been established by God. Romans 13:1

Faith Walk

Walk around a government building such as a city hall or county courthouse. What things about or around the building give you clues that important work happens inside?

Faith Talk

✧ What authorities has God placed in your life?

✧ What are the roles of these authorities? How does God show His love to you through them?

✧ According to today's passage, why should we honor earthly authorities?

✧ How can we honor and submit to them?

✧ How are we to respond when the government or other authorities (teachers, for example) ask us to behave in ways that are contrary to God's laws? (Read Daniel chapter 6 for an example.)

Follow-up Activities

✤ Make a habit of praying daily for different authorities such as the president or the police.

✤ Write a "Letter to the Editor" encouraging your community to honor its leaders.

✤ Write a thank you note to an outstanding leader in your community.

✤ Make several posters honoring the government and ask to put them up in public places such as the library.

✤ Make a donation of time or money to a public authority. Call and ask your police, mayor, or firefighters how you can be of service to them.

Our Response to God's Grace

Dear God, Heavenly Father,

You are Ruler of all. Thank You for giving us leaders to help our country, states, and cities run smoothly. Please raise up godly leaders for us and help us to follow the rules they give to us. Please forgive us when we fail to follow our leaders. In the name of Jesus, the King of kings. Amen.

Ponderings

✐ When Paul wrote the passage included here, the Roman rulers were pagan. His words mean that we are to submit and pay taxes to leaders even when they do not share our faith. What is your reaction to this passage?

✐ Are there times we should stop submitting to the government in order to keep God's laws? To study this issue further, read the following passages:

Matthew 22:15–22
    Should we pay taxes to a government that is using our money
    for evil purposes?

Daniel 1
    How should we respond when we are required to act
    against God's law?

Daniel 3 and Acts 5:27–32
    Whom should we put first in our lives?

Acts 5:30
    It is only by the power of the resurrected Christ that we are able to
    put God first in our lives.

↶ How can we honor our government while keeping God as our highest ruler?

↶ What are some issues or challenges we may face as we try to submit to the government while honoring God?

↶ Read Acts 16:22–34. What is the greatest gift we can give to those who are put in charge of us? How can we be a Paul and Silas in our day?

Journal Jottings

Lamb of God

God's Grace to Us

Today's Reading: John 1:19–34

The next day John saw Jesus coming toward him and said, "Look, the Lamb of God, who takes away the sin of the world!" John 1:29

Faith Walk

As you take a walk, look for ways sin has damaged the world (for example, litter along the road or graffiti on buildings). Look also for things about which God said, "It is good." For example, you might delight over a bird built perfectly for flight or examine the intricate designs of an evergreen tree.

Faith Talk

✧ Lent is a time to think about the sinfulness of the world and our own personal sinfulness. In what ways are you sinful?

✧ Sin has consequences. When you do something wrong, how are you punished?

✧ What are some of the results of sin you see in the world?

✧ Although pain, sadness, anger, and other problems came into the world because of sin, God did not forget His people. List the many ways God shows His love and grace to us daily. For example, He blesses us with food and clothing. He gives us laughter. And He gives us people who love us.

✧ God also came up with a plan to rescue us from the sin that people brought into the world. He sent a Savior, Jesus, to take the eternal punishment for our sins by dying on the cross. During Lent, the weeks before Easter, we focus on Christ's journey to the cross.

Follow-up Activities

✤ Write a list of family rules and consequences.

✤ Write a list of your sins. Tear it up. You are forgiven in Jesus. Your sins are gone.

✤ As a reminder of Christ giving up His life for you, give up something such as desserts or television for Lent.

✤ Make a beautiful creation such as a picture, poem, or sculpture. When you are finished, destroy it. How does destroying your creation make you feel? How do you think God felt when His perfect creation was destroyed by sin? But His story has a happy ending. Christ died to destroy sin and someday His creation will once again be perfect. Now make another new creation and keep it.

✤ Cut out a lamb (see Appendix B for a pattern) and write this week's Bible verse on it. Each night for a week say the words "Look, the Lamb of God who takes away the sin of the world!" together at bedtime or a mealtime.

Our Response to God's Grace

Dear Lord Jesus, Lamb of God,

Thank You for taking away our sins on the cross! Help us to go and sin no more. In Your forgiving name. Amen.

Ponderings

✐ Murders. Terrorism. Divorce. Poverty. Children rebelling. Disease. Death. It seems that sin and its consequences are overwhelming. But God has not sent the world to hell. Instead He sent Christ to hell to proclaim victory over Satan. "Look, the Lamb of God who takes away the sin of the world!" (John 1:29).

✐ Although Christ has been victorious over sin, the consequences of sin are evident daily in our lives. How has sin reared its ugly head in your life? God does not leave us hopeless, even in this life. Read Romans 8:28–39 for strength and reassurance.

- What are your pet sins? Make a practice of laying them daily at the foot of the cross.

- Look at yourself in the mirror. Now imagine looking at before-and-after pictures of your soul, before Christ's forgiveness and after His forgiveness.

- Read Romans 7:14–25. As Christians we struggle with sin. We are still sinful. But we are forgiven and desire to do that which is pleasing in God's sight. We are saints. Like Paul, we look at the cross of Christ and proclaim, "Thanks be to God—through Jesus Christ our Lord!"

Journal Jottings

Windy Weather

God's Grace to Us

Today's Reading: Mark 4:35–41

They were terrified and asked each other, "Who is this? Even the wind and waves obey Him!" Mark 4:41

Faith Walk

On a windy day, take a walk around your neighborhood looking for ways the wind makes its presence known (for example, waving tree branches and tinkling wind chimes). Try running with the wind and against the wind. Imagine God's power—stronger than the wind!

Faith Talk

✦ Reread the entire Scripture selection. Imagine the power of the wind and waves. Only God, the creator of the wind and the waves, has the power to make the wind stop and the waves be still. What does this story tell us about Jesus?

✦ What fears do you have? How can this story be a comfort?

✦ How does Jesus show His power in your life?

✦ Jesus' most powerful act was to win the fight against Satan when He died on the cross. If Jesus is powerful enough to stop sin, death, and the power of Satan, He is powerful enough to overcome all our fear!

✦ When friends or family members are worried or afraid, gently comfort them with a reminder of the power of God.

Follow-up Activities

❧ Look for man-made sources of wind in your home, such as a fan or a hair dryer. Use them to create a few moments of wind. After each yell, "Jesus is more powerful than the wind!"

❧ Act out the story of Jesus stilling the storm.

❧ Make wind chimes by hanging metal objects, such as nails and screws, from individual-sized pie tins. Hang your wind chimes outside on a windy day as a reminder of Jesus' strength.

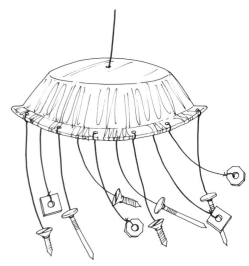

❧ Have fun in the wind. Blow bubbles. Which direction do they float? Fly paper airplanes with the wind and against the wind. What does it mean to be for God and against God?

❧ Finish the phrase, "Jesus is more powerful than ..."

Our Response to God's Grace

Dear Jesus,

You are more powerful than storms. You are more powerful than nightmares. You are more powerful than my greatest fears. Comfort me with Your power and help me to share Your strength with others. In Your powerful name. Amen.

Ponderings

❧ Reread Mark 4:35–41. The Sea of Galilee was in a basin surrounded by mountains and susceptible to sudden severe storms. Imagine the disciples' fear as their boat filled with water and tossed wildly about. What sudden storms have raged in your life? How did you handle them? In the light of this passage, would you handle them differently now? Why or why not?

❧ While this storm raged, Jesus was in the boat but was sound asleep. Where has Jesus been in the storms of your life?

- Why was Jesus sleeping? Read Luke 8:25 for a clue. Examine the storms in your life for the ways God tests and strengthens your faith.

- In the few short verses of this story, both the humanity and the deity of Jesus are revealed. The human Jesus, after a tiring day preaching to the crowds, escaped the masses and fell asleep, exhausted, in a boat. But Jesus is also God. He is in control. And with a few short words He quieted a raging storm. How can the duality of Jesus as both God and man be a comfort and strength for you in your life?

- Read in John 11:1–44 another example of Jesus as both God and man. Take comfort in a God who has felt your pain. Find strength in a God who is bigger than all the storms in your life, a God so big He even conquered death by His death on the cross.

Journal Jottings

Love in Action

God's Grace to Us

Today's Reading: 1 John 3:16–20

Dear children, let us not love with words or tongue but with actions and in truth. 1 John 3:18

Faith Walk

"Walk" the roads of those less fortunate in your community and share the love God has given you. Go to social agencies such as a food pantry or nursing home and talk to someone in charge to learn the needs of the people and how you can be of help to them.

Faith Talk

✧ Read all of 1 John 3:16–20. According to this passage, how do we know what love is?

✧ If God's love is in us, what does it compel us to do?

✧ Brainstorm ways you can demonstrate God's love to family, friends, and society.

✧ Create a family faith statement. Tell what you believe about God and describe ways He helps you put His love in action.

✧ Make a family plan for extending God's love to the community.

Follow-up Activities

❦ Put your plan for extending God's love into the community into action. Some possible ways to serve include stocking shelves at a food pantry, regularly visiting an elderly person, or offering to occasionally care for a disabled child to give the parents a break from this time-consuming responsibility.

✤ Do extra chores around the house to earn money for charity.

✤ Trace each person's hand, then color a red circle in the middle of each hand as a reminder of God's love in action: Jesus' death on the cross.

✤ Color pictures and write notes of encouragement that give witness to Jesus. Take them to a children's hospital or the children's wing of a hospital to be given to children who are suffering and need encouragement.

✤ Refer to the St. Valentine's Day lists activity in "Lay Down Your Life Love" (page 33) that show ways family members are made to feel loved, and continue to make a commitment to put your love into action in your family.

Our Response to God's Grace

Dear Jesus, Son of God,

Thank You for putting Your love into action on the cross that we might have the gift of eternal life. May the Holy Spirit work Your love in our hearts and lives so we might reach out to others in love. By the power of Your love. Amen.

Ponderings

✐ Read 1 John 3:11–4:21 and write, in your own words, an essay on love as outlined in these verses.

✐ Choose several portions of these verses from Scripture that speak to your heart and memorize them.

✐ Recall how God has demonstrated His love in your life. What has been your response? We are saved by faith, not by works. But faith brings us into a loving relationship with God. He loves us and we love Him. Because love is not merely a feeling but an action, faith drives us to respond to God's love through offerings, Bible study, and worship and to reach out to others through good deeds.

✒ Because loving relationships are nurtured through time spent together, make a commitment to spend regular time with God. Spend both scheduled times (worship, Bible study, prayer time) and unscheduled times (meditating on memorized Scripture as you drive, impromptu prayers, spontaneous faith conversations with others) with the Lord of your life. As you spend more time with God, He will grow His love in you.

✒ Spend time meditating on ways you can put God's love into practice in your life, pray for His help, and put them into action.

Journal Jottings

Take up the Cross

God's Grace to Us

Today's Reading: Mark 8:34–37

[Jesus said,] "If anyone would come after Me, he must deny himself and take up his cross and follow Me." Mark 8:34

Faith Walk

Play a game of "Follow the Leader." Designate a leader to lead everyone around the neighborhood. Have the leader lead through both tricky spots such as thick shrubbery and steep hills, and easy areas such as a smooth flat sidewalk or a momentary rest under a shade tree. Playing "Follow the Leader" can remind us to follow Jesus.

Faith Talk

✧ What was the hardest part of the walk? The easiest? How did you feel about those parts of the walk?

✧ What is the easiest part of being a Christian? The hardest? Why?

✧ In the Bible verse, what does God call us to do? What does that mean?

✧ Read Luke chapters 22–23. Jesus took up His cross and died for us. Why?

✧ How do you pick up your cross and follow God daily?

Follow-up Activities

❦ Get some ashes from a fireplace or have an adult burn paper to make ashes. Use the cooled ashes to make a cross on each person's forehead as a reminder that Jesus died so we won't die forever but live forever with Him in heaven.

✤ For supper one evening have a small serving of rice and water. Donate the money saved on the meal to a mission and pray for those people who don't know Christ as their Savior.

✤ Make bread crosses. Thaw frozen bread dough and let it rise according to the directions on the package. Shape fist-sized portions of dough into crosses. Bake as you would loaves of bread.

✤ Cut out a cross for each family member. (See page 285 in Appendix B for pattern.) Write the words to Mark 8:34 on the cross. Each night, for a week, read the verse together at the dinner table to help memorize it.

✤ Sing a Lenten song such as "Were You There When They Crucified My Lord?" or "There Is a Green Hill Far Away."

Our Response to God's Grace

Dear Jesus,

You took up Your cross and walked the road to Calvary, dying so we may have eternal life. Now, dear Lord, please help us take up our crosses and bear them out of love for You and for one another. In Your name. Amen.

Ponderings

꙳ What crosses has God placed in your life? What has been your reaction to those crosses? This Lenten season ponder the cross Christ bore for you. Pray for His help, comfort, and strength in bearing the crosses in your life.

꙳ Read Romans 5:3–4. Not only are we to pick up and bear our crosses but according to these verses, we are to rejoice in them. Why? What is the hope to which verse four refers?

꙳ During Lent, find more time to meditate on God's Word by choosing a day or meal each week to fast and spend that time reading the Bible and praying instead. Read the different accounts of the passion story as found in Matthew 26:14–27:56, Mark 14:12–15:41, Luke 22:1–23:49, and John 18:1–19:37.

🖊 Make a habit of confessing your sins to God daily. Write them down. Ask His forgiveness. Then tear up the paper and throw it away, knowing that your sins are forgiven and the guilt has been removed from you. Go and sin no more.

🖊 Pray for your children. Ask God to help them to always remember the cross Christ bore for them and to faithfully bear any crosses they may be given. Seek His strength for them when they face temptations to deny their faith or live contrary to what they have been taught. Pray for His help in guiding you as a Christian parent.

Journal Jottings

March

march

Lions and Lambs

God's Grace to Us

Today's Reading: Isaiah 11:1–9

The wolf will live with the lamb, the leopard will lie down with the goat, the calf and the lion and the yearling together; and a little child will lead them. Isaiah 11:6

Faith Walk

Take walks on two different days—a "good" weather day and a "bad" weather day. Compare the two walks. Which one did you like more?

Faith Talk

✧ In early spring, the weather changes frequently and sometimes rapidly. That is why the phrase "March: in like a lion, out like a lamb" is used. What is the difference between a "lion day" and a "lamb day"?

✧ How are real lions and real lambs different from each other?

✧ In the Bible verse, Isaiah paints a picture of peace among the animal kingdoms and people. This is the peace brought by Jesus' death on the cross and which we will experience in heaven. What is peace?

✧ This picture of God's kingdom is much like God's kingdom before the fall of sin in the Garden of Eden. How are heaven and the Garden of Eden similar?

✧ In Revelation, heaven is described as a city of jewels with the river of the water of life running through the middle of it and the glory of God shining brighter than the sun. What does this description tell you about heaven?

Follow-up Activities

✤ For the remainder of the month, keep a record of "lion" and "lamb" days.

✤ Make a diorama (three-dimensional scene) of heaven using a shoe box and items you can find.

✤ Close your eyes and imagine heaven as each family member takes turns describing it in their own words.

✤ Visit a pet store. Interview someone at the store to learn more about the animals.

✤ Visit a jewelry store. As you look at the precious stones, imagine the riches and beauty of heaven.

Our Response to God's Grace

Dear God our Father, Lord of Heaven and Earth,

You are preparing a place for us in heaven, a place filled with all good and wonderful things, especially Your glory. When we have pain, sadness, or trouble, help us to focus on what You have done for us through Christ, picturing heaven and remembering that someday we will no longer have the hurts and problems of this world. In His saving name. Amen.

Ponderings

✐ The sword of sin is divisive. It separates us from the love of God—we cannot see and commune with Him face to face. It separates us from one another—we say hurtful things, doubt each other's love, and struggle to have intimacy. It rips apart the unity of the natural world—a raging hurricane destroys a coastal area, a lion preys on a lamb, a mosquito drinks someone's blood, a fire destroys a forest. How have you seen the divisiveness of sin in your life?

✐ In this sin-ridden world of pain and suffering, God has not deserted us. The sun rises, casting a golden hue on the day. A doctor successfully performs a life-saving operation. A family enjoys a vacation. A lonely widow finds comfort in prayer. How have you experienced God's abundance in your life?

No, God has not deserted us. He has always provided a shining ray of hope. At the fall of man in the Garden of Eden, God told the serpent He would send an offspring of man to crush his head (a prophecy of the Savior). In the flood He kept the hope alive by saving a remnant, Noah and his family. And at the death of Christ, the hope foretold became a reality. Yes, we have a shining ray of hope.

At the end of the world, Jesus will separate the sheep (the faithful) from the goats (the faithless). The faithless will be eternally separated from God and thrown into everlasting darkness. For them there will be no more hope. The sword of sin will divide them for all eternity.

The faithful, cleansed by the blood of Jesus, will be returned to a state of perfection for eternity. There will be no more sword of sin, no more division. God's glory and love will reign and the lion will lie down with the lamb. Yes, we have hope!

Journal Jottings

Silent Prayer Walk

God's Grace to Us

Today's Reading: John 17:1–26

After Jesus said this, He looked toward heaven and prayed. John 17:1

Faith Walk

Take a silent walk. Rather than talking to one another, pray silently, talking to God your Father.

Faith Talk

✧ As Jesus prepared for His death, He turned to His Father and spent some quiet time in prayer.

✧ Jesus prayed for Himself, that God would glorify Him through His death.

✧ Jesus prayed for His disciples, that God would protect them, unify them, and give them joy.

✧ Jesus prayed for all believers, that God would unify them, that God's love be in them, and that they be with Jesus.

✧ During Lent, we can focus on prayer as a way to better know God's love given to us in Jesus' death.

Follow-up Activities

❦ Try praying in different positions: kneeling, prostrate (lying down), hands folded, arms raised up to heaven, or arms crossed like pretzels.

❦ Early believers sometimes prayed with their arms crossed like pretzels. Make pretzels from bread dough as a reminder of the relationship we can have with God through prayer.

- ♣ Glue six store-bought pretzels into a cross shape as a reminder that Jesus prayed for us, God's children before His death on the cross.

- ♣ Start a prayer journal. Record your prayers and periodically go back through your journal and write God's answers to your prayers.

- ♣ Make a book of family prayers. Write out and illustrate each memorized prayer your family uses.

Our Response to God's Grace

Dear Jesus, our Savior,

Thank You for Your great love for us as revealed in Your prayers before Your death. May the power of the Holy Spirit in our hearts bring us to You in prayer so our faith may be strengthened. In Your name. Amen.

Ponderings

- ❧ Jesus prayed for Himself. Reread John 17:1–5. During Lent we usually focus on Christ the Suffering Servant. But these verses speak of Christ glorified through His death. Paraphrase these verses in your own words.

- ❧ Jesus prayed for His disciples. Reread John 17:6–19. These verses reveal the deep, intimate love Jesus felt for His disciples. Use these passages to write a description of Christ's relationship with His disciples.

- ❧ Jesus prayed for all believers. Reread verses 20–26. It is you Christ is praying for in these verses! What kind of a relationship does Christ desire to have with you?

- ❧ Prayer is communion with God. This is the longest prayer of Christ recorded in the Bible and the theme that runs throughout this prayer is one of unity, union, communion. Reflect on this tender, loving example of communion with God that the Holy Spirit presents as a gift to all believers.

- ❧ Read and meditate on Romans 8:26–27. This passage describes a very intimate relationship between the prayers of saints and the Spirit of God.

Journal Jottings

Three-in-One

God's Grace to Us

Today's Reading: Matthew 3:16–17

As soon as Jesus was baptized, He went up out of the water. At that moment heaven was opened, and He saw the Spirit of God descending like a dove and lighting on Him. And a voice from heaven said, "This is My Son, whom I love; with Him I am well pleased." Matthew 3:16–17

Faith Walk

Take a walk looking for examples of three-in-one. For example, you might look for three-leaf clovers, trees (roots, wood, and leaves), houses (foundation, walls, and roof), or a river (the banks, the bed, and the water).

Faith Talk

✧ God is Three-in-One. He is three Persons—the Father, the Son, and the Holy Spirit—yet one God.

✧ God the Father is the Creator. He created the heavens, the earth, and everything in them.

✧ God the Son—Jesus—is the Savior. By His death on the cross, He saved us from sin and gave us heaven.

✧ God the Holy Spirit creates faith in our hearts and guides us in our lives.

✧ The March holiday, St. Patrick's Day, was created to honor St. Patrick, a missionary to Ireland. St. Patrick brought tens of thousands of people to faith in Jesus as their Savior. He taught them about the Trinity—God as Three-in-One—using the three-leaf clover as an example.

Follow-up Activities

🍁 Make three-leaf clovers:

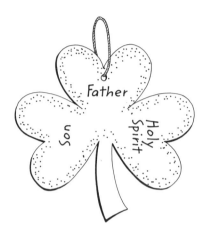

1. Cut a clover from green construction paper using the pattern in Appendix B.

2. On each leaf write the name of one of the Persons in the Trinity. Decorate the edges of the leaves with green glitter.

3. Punch a hole in the top and tie a yarn loop through each clover. Hang them on your bedroom doorknobs as a reminder of the Holy Trinity's work in your lives.

🍁 Draw symbols for the Trinity (i.e. a triangle). Each symbol must have three parts but be a whole.

🍁 Cut open one or more apples and examine the three parts (seeds, meat, and skin). Read the book *3 in One* by Joanne Marxhausen (Concordia Publishing House, 1973). Have a delicious snack of apple slices.

🍁 Celebrate the unity of your family by making family sweatshirts. Create a logo and slogan and paint them on white sweatshirts. Have everyone wear the sweatshirts for a family outing.

🍁 Just as the Father, Son, and Holy Spirit have unique roles, each person in the family plays a unique role. On a sheet of paper, list each family member and their roles. Take turns thanking God for the blessings of every family member.

Our Response to God's Grace

Dear Triune God—Father, Son, and Holy Spirit,

You are a mystery—three yet one. You are the Father Creator, the Savior Son, and the Faith-Giving Holy Spirit. Together You make up one complete God, who can do anything. Praise and thanks to You. In the name of the Triune God. Amen.

Ponderings

🖋 In John 1:1–2 Christ is called the Word. Read Genesis 1:1–3. Pay close attention to the words "created," "Spirit of God," and "said." Together what do these passages tell us about the presence and roles of the Holy Trinity at creation?

🖋 Read Job 38:1–41:11. Waters bursting forth, the joyous shouts of angels, mountain goats giving birth, lionesses hunting prey, the powerful behemoth and terrifying leviathan, the footings of the earth and the constellations of the sky all speak of the power of God, the Creator, Owner, and Keeper of all.

🖋 Read Romans 5:6–11. Study, ponder, and memorize this passage. Rewrite it in your own words. What does it say about God the Savior and His relationship to us?

🖋 Study Romans 8:1–17. Using these verses, write an explanation of the role of the Holy Spirit in our lives.

🖋 Research the life of St. Patrick, the Christian martyr who worked to break Satan's hold over Ireland by proclaiming the Gospel and who used a simple shamrock to teach the mysteries of the Trinity.

Journal Jottings

Signs of the End Times

God's Grace to Us

Today's Reading: Matthew 24:1–35*

[Jesus said,] "Now learn this lesson from the fig tree: As soon as its twigs get tender and its leaves come out, you know that summer is near. Even so, when you see these things, you know that it is near, right at the door." Matthew 24:32

Faith Walk

Take a walk around your neighborhood, looking for signs of the coming spring.

Faith Talk

✧ Jesus' death and resurrection were the beginning of the end times. Our Savior has come and taken away our sins. Now, in the end times, we wait for Him to come a second time to take all believers with Him to heaven.

✧ Just like we can see signs of spring coming, we can also see signs of Jesus coming back.

✧ There will be earthquakes, wars, and famine. People will falsely claim that they are Christ. Through it all, God's Holy Spirit will be with believers, strengthening and guiding them.

✧ At the end of time, Jesus will return to take believers home with Him to heaven.

✧ It is because Jesus died on the cross, taking the punishment for our sins, that we will be able to live with Him in heaven.

* Some of the material in these verses may be very frightening for young children. Please pre-read this section and determine what your child is able to handle. It also important to emphasize that God is with believers in the most difficult situations.

Follow-up Activities

♣ Take photographs of the "signs of spring" you see in your yard or neighborhood.

♣ Write a newspaper article as if you were a reporter covering Jesus' Second Coming.

♣ Imagine what you think heaven will be like and color a picture of it.

♣ Play "Sizzle!" Make a circle with one person in the middle blindfolded. Pass a ball around. When the person in the middle yells "Sizzle!" the person holding the ball is "burned." The players in the circle know the word "Sizzle!" will be called, but they don't know when. In the same way, we know Christ will return, but we don't know when. We need to be faithful at all times.

♣ Put a spring twig on your family altar as a reminder to watch for Christ's Second Coming.

Our Response to God's Grace

Dear Jesus, Savior of the World,

As we ponder Your death and wait with joy for Your return, we ask that You keep us strong in faith. In Your name. Amen.

Ponderings

🖎 Reread the Scripture passage. Write a list of the "signs" of which Jesus speaks. Which of these signs do you see happening in modern times? What is the significance of these signs?

🖎 Read verses 36 to the end of the chapter. We cannot know when Christ will return. God wants us to have faith in Christ's second return and the discipleship that comes with watching and waiting. How can you better watch and wait for Christ's Second Coming in your life?

🖎 Read Matthew 25:1–13. Many people will be spiritually unprepared for Christ's return. It is easy to get complacent and forget the urgency that these chapters proclaim. Christ could return at any moment. It is urgent that we immediately proclaim Christ to those who do not know Him. Invite those you know who do not yet believe to join you as you worship, inviting them to see God revealed.

✍ Read verses 14–30. These verses prophesy the horrors that would occur when Jerusalem was destroyed as well as the horrors that will occur as the end of the world approaches. They also speak of hope, the hope that all who believe in Christ as their Savior have in His return. The horrors will end and Jesus will come again with power and glory.

✍ Read verses 31–46. In these verses, Christ returns and separates the faithful from the faithless. For those without faith, every misdeed and inaction is recalled. For the faithful, only their good deeds are remembered. God gives us an inheritance, a kingdom, prepared for us—eternal life!

Journal Jottings

Muddy Day Madness

God's Grace to Us

Today's Reading: Psalm 40:1–3

He lifted me out of the slimy pit, out of the mud and mire; He set my feet on a rock and gave me a firm place to stand. Psalm 40:2

Faith Walk

Put on grubby clothes and take a walk outside on a muddy day. Experience some muddy day madness. Stomp in the mud. Touch it with your hands. Squish it. Relish the experience.

Faith Talk

✧ What does the mud feel like? What would happen if you jumped into a really deep puddle of mud or drove a car into it?

✧ Have you ever sunk low into the mud in your life? For example, have you struggled in school, been sick or hurt, or gotten into a bad fight with someone you care about? Tell about your experience.

✧ Read all three verses of the passage. What was David's experience?

✧ How can these verses help us when we're hurting inside?

✧ What hope do these verses give us?

Follow-up Activities

✿ Look for sticky substances in your home (for example, cookie dough, glue, and syrup). Touch and describe each substance. What sticky situations are in your life? How can you keep from getting permanently stuck to them?

✿ Pray for someone who is experiencing a low point in his or her life.

🍁 Plant a seed in some mud. God can plant hope in the mud in our lives and grow it into a beautiful plant.

🍁 Write your own psalm about God's work in your life.

🍁 Make a care package for a homeless person. Contact a local homeless shelter for ideas of what to include in the package. Add a note of encouragement and a witness of your faith as a part of the package.

Our Response to God's Grace

Dear God the Father, Lord of all Heights,

When I fly high with the joy of Your love, You rejoice with me and cheer me on. When I feel low and hurt, You hold me, comfort me, and give me hope. Help me to know Your presence and love at all times. In the name of Jesus. Amen.

Ponderings

🌾 Read all of Psalm 40. In this psalm how does God use David to teach us about God's character, His relationship to us, prayer, and life difficulties?

🌾 Many times God seems far away as we cry out in pain, "Where are You, God?" But God is not far away. He hears our cry. He feels our pain. Knowing this, we can wait patiently for Him to lift us out of the mud and mire. A God who knows the number of hairs on our head; who walked the earth and knew tiredness, hunger, grief, and pain; a perfect God who suffered agony on the cross and died for the most evil of sinners is surely a God of love who tenderly carries us through our darkest days.

🌾 Why does God allow His precious children to suffer pain? To help answer this question read Romans 5:3–5 and Job 42:3.

🌾 When we are hurting, how can we pray? In this psalm-prayer David recalls God's past acts of grace. He praises God for His righteousness and blessings. He repents of his sins and in faith he cries out and pleads with the Lord for help.

🌾 How can this psalm be a source of comfort, encouragement, and guidance in the mire and mud in your life?

Journal Jottings

Walkin' in the Rain

God's Grace to Us

Today's Reading: The Book of Jude

They are clouds without rain, blown along by the wind. Jude 12b

Faith Walk

Take a walk outside on a rainy day. If the weather is warm, walk without rain gear and feel the wetness. How does it feel to walk in the rain?

Faith Talk

✧ Why is rain good? Imagine a world without rain. What would happen?

✧ This week's Bible verse compares false teachers to clouds without rain. They promise good things but leave people spiritually thirsty for God.

✧ Read John 4:13–14. Jesus tells us that He is the water that keeps us from being thirsty. When we drink of the forgiveness Jesus offers, we will thirst no more!

✧ What can we do to offer spiritual water—the love of Jesus and His forgiveness—to others?

Follow-up Activities

❧ Grow or buy two small plants. Do the following experiment: Water one plant diligently; let the other plant dry up. Compare the two plants to people with and without the forgiveness Jesus offers.

❧ Pour a glass of ice water for each family member and have a toast to Jesus, the Living Water.

❧ Take turns using a spray bottle to spray water in one another's faces. Each time you spray water say, "Jesus is the Living Water."

✤ Play "Truth or Fiction." Have each family member take turns being "It" and telling three statements of "fact." Two statements should be true, one false. Those who aren't "It" must guess which statement is false. Sometimes knowing what is true is tricky. That is why it is easy to follow false religious leaders. To know God's truth we must read and study the Bible.

✤ Fill an empty bottle with water. Label it "Living Water." Place it on your home altar as a reminder to drink from the well of Jesus' forgiveness.

Our Response to God's Grace

Dear Jesus,

You are the Living Water, our source of eternal life. Help us, by the power of Your Spirit, to share Your love and forgiveness with those who thirst. Keep us alert for false teachers and show us the truth through Your Word. In Your power. Amen.

Ponderings

✍ Read the whole book of Jude. Jude's greatest desire was to write about salvation through Jesus. Instead he found himself having to write a letter warning the church to be alert for false prophets passing themselves off as believers. How is this a threat to the Church today?

✍ Verses 3–16 describe the characteristics of false teachers. How can we tell the difference between a true prophet of God and someone Satan has planted in the Church to draw us away from the true faith?

✍ Verses 20–21 are keys to how we can protect ourselves against false prophets. What are the keys?

✍ As true believers we are also called to be prophets to those around us. This role is explained in verses 22–23. It is an impossible task, apart from the Holy Spirit, to discern which people need to hear of God's love for us in Jesus. Pray for the Holy Spirit's guidance as you reach out to others with the Word of God and the Living Water, Jesus Christ. Keep in your prayers those individuals you know are spiritually lost, wandering, or confused.

✍ The doxology in verses 24–25 is both a reminder of the grace and strength we have in Christ Jesus, our Savior, and a hymn of praise to the one true God. Memorize these verses, and when faced with struggles to remain faithful, pull them out as a sword against Satan.

Journal Jottings

April

april

Tree Branch Parade

God's Grace to Us

Today's Reading: Mark 11:1–11

"Hosanna! Blessed is He who comes in the name of the Lord! Blessed is the coming kingdom of our father David! Hosanna in the highest!" Mark 11:9b–10

Faith Walk

Take a walk and pick up fallen branches and leaves. At home, lay them in a path in your yard as a tribute to Christ the King.

Faith Talk

✧ Read the whole Scripture passage. What does this story tell us about Jesus?

✧ The people praised Jesus as their King. How can you praise Jesus as your King?

✧ This story begins Holy Week, which ends with Jesus' death and resurrection.

✧ Jesus knew that the people would praise Him as the Messiah (Savior), which would make the church leaders angry and lead to His death, yet He rode into town anyway. Why?

✧ Jesus rode into Jerusalem on a young donkey. The donkey represented gentleness, peace, humility, and royalty (in the Old Testament donkeys were used by royalty, including King David). How do these qualities reflect the character of Jesus?

Follow-up Activities

❧ Cut palm branches from paper (pattern in Appendix B) and write the people's words of praise on them. Hang the palm branches in a prominent place and recite the words daily as a worship activity.

❧ Act out the Bible story, using a broom for a donkey and jackets and tree branches for the path.

❧ Write a family song of praise that speaks of Jesus as your Savior. Set it to a familiar tune such as "The Farmer in the Dell" or "Twinkle, Twinkle, Little Star."

❧ Praise God with bells as you sing a favorite praise song.

❧ Read all four accounts of this story as found in Matthew 21:1–11, Mark 11:1–11, Luke 19:28–44, and John 12:12–19. Write a "newspaper article" chronicling the events and discussing their importance. Save the article to put together with other articles written in future weeks.

Our Response to God's Grace

Dear Savior, Messiah, King,

Hosanna in the highest! You came to bring us the kingdom promised to David—the kingdom of heaven! We praise You for Your glorious gift! In Your saving name. Amen.

Ponderings

✐ Read all four passages listed above. Make a list of what these passages reveal to us about Jesus.

✐ Continue to study the significance of these events by reading the following passages:

Zechariah 9:9–10—The triumphal entry is prophesied
Numbers 19:2—Flawless animals are used for religious reasons
2 Kings 9:13—A mule is the transportation of a king
2 Kings 9:13—The arrival of a king is announced
2 Samuel 7:11b–14—God promises to establish His kingdom through David

✐ Every word in the Old Testament was inspired by God to foreshadow the New Testament and to proclaim salvation. How do these passages fulfill that role?

✐ Jesus, like a never-harnessed colt, was perfect, without sin. Yet by riding into Jerusalem on a donkey, He proclaimed Himself Messiah and nailed His fate to the sinner's cross. What an awesome God!

✐ Christ was a sacrificial king—exalted above all others, yet as low as a thief on a cross. How can this dual role be a comfort and strength to you?

Journal Jottings

A Stroll through a Garden

God's Grace to Us

Today's Reading: Matthew 26:17–56

Jesus replied, "Friend, do what you came for." Then the men stepped forward, seized Jesus and arrested Him. Matthew 26:50

Faith Walk

Stroll through your neighborhood looking for gardens. Which ones are your favorites?

Faith Talk

✧ When you look at or think about gardens, what thoughts go through your mind?

✧ Gardens usually represent peace, beauty, wealth, and life. But in the Garden of Gethsemane, the quietness of the night was interrupted by the arrest of Jesus.

✧ When Jesus walked through the Garden of Gethsemane at Passover, it wasn't just a stroll through a garden. Jesus came to Gethsemane knowing He would be arrested.

✧ Because of Jesus' arrest, death, and resurrection, we can have peace knowing our sins are forgiven.

✧ At the Garden of Gethsemane, we received beauty—the beauty of God's great love, wealth—the rich gift of forgiveness, and life—the promise of eternal life in heaven.

Follow-up Activities

❦ Plant a garden, indoors or out, as a reminder of the blessings we have received from Jesus.

- Create a spot outside to sit and think about Jesus. It might be a large rock, a lawn swing under the shade of a tree, or any other quiet spot you can create.
- Visit a botanical garden or a beautifully sculptured city park. Compare it to Gethsemane.
- Loosely tie yarn around both wrists and imagine being Jesus and having your wrists tied together as you are led away to your death.
- Write a news account of the Maundy Thursday events and add it to your Palm Sunday news story.

Our Response to God's Grace

Dear Jesus,

Because the quietness of the garden was broken by the turmoil of Your arrest, the troubles of our lives can be broken by the peace of Your forgiveness. Help us turn to You for help when we need forgiveness and comfort from pain. For Your sake we pray. Amen.

Ponderings

- The Garden of Gethsemane was a quiet place where Jesus could go to spend time with His Father. But it was also a place of passion, reflecting His passion. Gethsemane means "olive press." In New Testament times, the olive press was a heavy stone or board that smashed the oil out of the olives. The Garden of Gethsemane, the olive press, foreshadowed the agony of Christ in which His blood would be pressed or poured out from His body.
- The olive trees, gnarled and frightening looking, also remind us of the agony Christ was going through.
- Jesus was arrested during the Passover festival. During the festival, thousands of animals were sacrificed and their blood drained. The blood was funneled into a ditch leading down to the Kidron Valley. When Jesus crossed the Kidron Valley to go to the Garden of Gethsemane, He would have crossed a river of flowing blood. Imagine His passion, His agony as He crossed the river of sacrificial blood knowing that soon His blood also would be sacrificed.

❧ Jesus' agony in the garden was excruciating. He cried out in despair to His Father. His sweat was like tears of blood. In humiliation, He allowed sinners to arrest Him, the blameless King of the universe, and lead Him like a lamb to slaughter.

❧ Christ's agony, unbearable though it may seem, was also one of triumph, for as He was led away, the sins of the world were also led away with Him. In John 18:11 Jesus says, "Shall I not drink the cup the Father has given Me?" Christ's passion was a triumph for Him—He won the war against Satan. It was a triumph for us—our sins were removed from us. And Christ's passion was a triumph for the Father—He had sent Jesus; His will was done.

Journal Jottings

Good! Friday

God's Grace to Us

Today's Reading: John 19:17–37

When He had received the drink, Jesus said, "It is finished." With that, He bowed His head and gave up His spirit. John 19:30

Faith Walk

Take a silent, no talking, walk. Use the time to think about the events of Good Friday. Think about why Good Friday was both a terrible day and a good day.

Faith Talk

✧ Before your walk, read through the whole Scripture selection and talk about the events of Good Friday.

✧ Focus on what Jesus must have been feeling as He was condemned to death, physically abused, and finally crucified.

✧ When Jesus said "It is finished" and died, it was a sad moment for His followers. Their beloved Jesus was dead and their hearts were broken. What the disciples didn't know was that the words, "It is finished," were the most beautiful, joyful words ever spoken. "It is finished," meant not only that the crucifixion was over and Jesus was dead, but also that God's plan of salvation was finished. God's children were free from sin and death!

✧ Jesus gave up His spirit to death and to life for us! Praise the Lord!

Follow-up Activities

❈ In the evening, sit together in a darkened room, hold hands, and pray for help in spreading the news of Jesus' death. Pray for pastors and missionaries who diligently work to spread this news to unbelievers.

- Hang a large nail in a prominent place as a reminder that our sins were nailed to the cross.
- Make crucifixion banners:

    Jesus' blood shed for me

    1. Paint handprints on pieces of felt.
    2. After they dry paint the palms red.
    3. Add the words "Jesus' blood shed for me."
    4. Punch holes at the top of the banners, add string, and hang.
- Make a crucifixion bag:
    1. Place objects pertaining to the Good Friday story in a bag. Objects to use can include a purple cloth, a stick, thorns, rope, coins, a cross, and nails.
    2. Take turns drawing objects out of the bag and using them to tell about the Good Friday story.
- Add the story of Good Friday to your newspaper articles.

Our Response to God's Grace

Precious Jesus,

It is finished. Your work on earth is done. As You bowed Your head and died, Your sacrifice was complete. Because You cried out in pain, we can cry out in joy. For this, O Lord, we thank You. In Your forgiving name. Amen.

Ponderings

- Read all four passion narratives as found in Matthew 26:14–27:66, Mark 14:12–15:47, Luke 22:1–23:56, and John 18:1–19:42. What jumps out at you from these passages?
- Jesus' passion and death is filled with symbolic meaning. Read very carefully Matthew 27:51. The curtain that tore separated the Holy Place from the Most Holy Place. The Most Holy Place, or Holy of Holies, was so sacred that

only the high priest could go into it and only once a year, on the day of atonement. When the curtain tore from top to bottom, Christ tore down the barrier between God and us. Christ had atoned for our sins for all time. We were given direct access to an intimate relationship with God.

✎ Read verses 52–53. This incident is found only in the book of Matthew. Christ had not only torn down the barriers between God and man, He also conquered death.

✎ In your mind, picture Jesus' death. Three hours prior to His death darkness covered the sky. At the time of Jesus' death there was an earthquake. Jesus, the true Sacrificial Lamb, died at the moment the Passover lamb was being slaughtered. In the words of the centurion, "Surely He was the Son of God!"

✎ Why can the story of Jesus' death be called the climax of the Bible?

Journal Jottings

New Life Easter

God's Grace to Us

Today's Reading: John 20:1–31

But these are written that you may believe that Jesus is the Christ, the Son of God, and that by believing you may have life in His name. John 20:31

Faith Walk

Take a walk looking for the springtime signs of new life. For example, a budding tree, a blooming flower, a newborn animal, or a baby bird.

Faith Talk

✧ Read all of John 20 and make a list of all of the moments of joy.

✧ John 14:6 says, "Jesus answered, 'I am the Way, the Truth, and the Life. No one comes to the Father except through Me.'" What did Jesus mean?

✧ What is the new life that we have through Jesus?

✧ Not only do we receive a new life through Jesus but, because of Jesus, we are new creations. We are made clean and perfect, and with Jesus' help we live a newly created life of goodness.

✧ How can we live as new creations?

Follow-up Activities

❦ Have a resurrection celebration. Play joyful Easter music. Celebrate with flowers and balloons. Eat cake and ice cream and drink punch.

❦ Have a family sing-along of favorite Easter songs.

❦ Catch a new life—a spring bug—in a jar. Add grass, a leaf, a twig, and some drops of water to the jar. Watch your bug for a while before releasing it back into the wild.

❦ Start a sticker book of new life stickers such as butterflies, chicks, caterpillars, or flowers.

❦ Write a news article of the Easter story. Combine all the news articles into a mini newspaper, photocopy the paper, and pass copies to neighbors and friends.

Our Response to God's Grace

Dear Resurrected Lord,

You are risen. You are risen indeed. Alleluia! You have given to us a new life of hope, peace, and joy. Help us to live our lives as new creations in You. By Your risen power we pray. Amen.

Ponderings

✐ Read Genesis chapter three. Write a description of the results of sin.

✐ Read 1 Corinthians 15:20–28 and 42–57. Write a description of the results of Christ's resurrection.

✐ Read 1 Corinthians 15:58. What is to be our response to the victory Christ has given us? How, by the power of Jesus, can you live out that response in your life?

✐ We are both the Old Adam—sinners, and the New Adam—saints. Christ has made us forgiven and perfect in the sight of God, but we are not yet perfect in our actions, we still commit sins. In Romans 7:14–25 Paul discusses the struggle he has with the nature of sin still in him. How does the Old Adam of sin manifest itself in your life?

✐ In Romans 8:1–17, Paul continues by describing life in the Spirit. How do you see yourself as a new creation? Praise be to Jesus Christ for taking the rotting spirit within us and turning it into a new and glorious creation!

Journal Jottings

Blindfolded

God's Grace to Us

Today's Reading: John 21:1–22

Jesus answered, "If I want him to remain alive until I return, what is that to you? You must follow Me." John 21:22

Faith Walk

Take turns leading one another around the neighborhood blindfolded. Be extra alert and be on the lookout for traffic, curbs, and other things that could be dangerous.

Faith Talk

✧ What does it feel like to be led around blindfolded?

✧ When you are blindfolded, you must trust the person who is leading you. What does it mean to trust someone else?

✧ Jesus told Peter, "Follow Me." What do you think He meant?

✧ Jesus wants us to trust Him and follow Him in our lives. Peter failed the first time he was to follow Jesus. When Jesus was on trial, Peter lied and said he didn't know Jesus. When Jesus rose from the dead, Peter was forgiven and Jesus welcomed him back. Like Peter, we sometimes fail to follow Jesus but, because He rose, we too can be welcomed back. How can we follow Jesus in our lives?

✧ Jesus asked Peter, "Do you love Me?" It is because we love Jesus that we follow Him.

Follow-up Activities

♣ Play a game of "Follow the Leader."

♣ Write a list of ways you trust your family members. Write another list of ways you trust Jesus.

♣ One way the disciples were called on to trust Jesus was to throw their nets back into the water after a night of fishing with no results. Go fishing and think of the blessings Jesus showered on His disciples.

♣ Jesus asked Peter to follow Him by feeding His lambs—feeding the Word of God to others. Find a way to feed the Word of God to someone who needs it through a note, a music tape, or a phone call.

♣ Cut a pair of footprints (see Appendix B for a pattern) for each family member. Write your names on them and make a path as a reminder to follow Jesus.

Our Response to God's Grace

Dear Jesus, whom I love,

Help me to trust in You and to follow You in all the footsteps of my life, knowing that You love me as my Savior. Through the power of Your name. Amen.

Ponderings

☙ Write an answer to the question, "What does it mean to follow Jesus?"

☙ As you read each of the following passages, jot down what each passage says about following the Lord:

Exodus 23:2
Leviticus 18:3
2 Chronicles 34:29–33; Numbers 13:1–30 and 14:24
Matthew 4:18–20
Matthew 8:18–22 and Luke 9:23–24
Hebrews 12:1–3

☙ In what ways have you been led to follow God in your life? Do you always know where God is leading you?

- In what ways could you better follow Jesus?

- Spend some time in prayer and meditation reflecting on what it means to follow Jesus. Write, once again, an answer to the question "What does it mean to follow Jesus?" Pray for the Holy Spirit's help as you journey in the footsteps of Jesus and when, like Peter, you fail, pray for the forgiveness that can be found in Christ.

Journal Jottings

Arbor Day Habitat Hunt

God's Grace to Us

Today's Reading: Psalm 1

He is like a tree planted by streams of water, which yields its fruit in season. Psalm 1:3a

Faith Walk

Walk through a neighborhood or park that has a multitude of trees. Try to identify as many trees as possible and examine the habitats in which they are located.

Faith Talk

✧ In the spring many people are busy planting—gardens, flowers, bushes, grasses, and trees.

✧ The last Friday of April is Arbor Day, a day in which people are encouraged to plant trees.

✧ Trees are considered to be a symbol of life. The green leaves and flowers or fruits of some trees remind us that they are living. Trees also give life—they provide food, shelter, and fuel, and they improve the air and water quality. Evergreen trees remind us of everlasting life.

✧ Trees cannot live alone. They need a good environment in which to live and grow. Trees need water, sunshine, air, and nutrients from the soil to grow and become healthy, productive trees.

✧ People, like trees, need a fertile spiritual environment to live and grow in the faith and become healthy, productive children of God. We need the nourishment we receive from being rooted in God's Word. We need to study the Bible, attend church, make Christian friends and mentors, and be involved with Bible studies and devotions.

Follow-up Activities

✤ Plant a tree. For sources of free or inexpensive trees, go to the web site http://www.arborday.com and click on "free trees."

✤ Cut open several varieties of fruits and examine them. How are they alike? How are they different?

✤ Walk through a supermarket and look at the fruit. Determine which fruits are good and which are bad (beginning to rot).

✤ People also produce good or bad fruits. To produce good fruits, a person must be rooted and fed in the faith. Write a list of ways your faith is fed (for example, Bible study or singing hymns). Pick one item from your list and commit to nurturing it for a week. At the end of the week, discuss your experience.

✤ Drink only water for a day as a reminder that those who are rooted in God's Word—the source of Living Water—bear good fruit.

Our Response to God's Grace

Dear Jesus, Living Water,

Help us to be nourished by Your Word. Strengthen us by the power of the Holy Spirit to bear good fruit for You and Your kingdom. In the name of Jesus, the Word. Amen.

Ponderings

✆ Examine yourself. Are you rooted in God's Word? What fruits do you bear? How can you become more like a tree planted by streams of living water? Pray for God's wisdom and His help in strengthening your faith.

✆ Examine your family. How rooted has it been in God's Word? What fruits have you noticed your family bearing? Pray for the Lord's wisdom and help in strengthening your family's faith.

✒ Read Ephesians 6:10–18. In this passage, God's Word is a sword. Why is God's Word described in Psalm 1 as something that brings life and here in Ephesians as a tool of destruction?

✒ Write a psalm describing the spiritual wholeness that comes from being planted in the soil of God's Word.

Journal Jottings

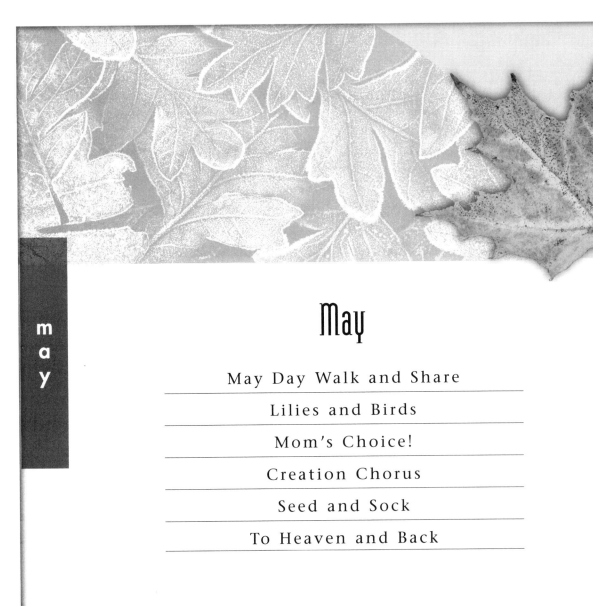

May

may

May Day Walk and Share

God's Grace to Us

Today's Reading: Matthew 25:31–46

"The King will reply, 'I tell you the truth, whatever you did for one of the least of these brothers of Mine, you did for Me.'" Matthew 25:40

Faith Walk

Take a May Day walk around your neighborhood or in a nursing home and handout treats. Treats may include bookmarks, cut flowers, or homemade cards. With each May Day treat, include a letter witnessing your faith and wishing the recipient a blessed May Day. If you go to a nursing home, clear your visit with a supervisor or administrator.

Faith Talk

✧ Read the whole discourse of "The Sheep and the Goats" found in the Scripture reading. Why does Jesus say that when we do something kind for even the "least" of people, we are doing it for Him?

✧ What things does Jesus say we are to do for Him by doing for others?

✧ When Jesus is the Master, the God of our lives, we love Him and want to serve Him. When He returns, He will remember that we served Him. If we do not love Jesus, when He returns, He will remember only our sin.

✧ For those who love and serve Jesus without thought of receiving a reward, but instead because He first loved us, God promises an inheritance of eternal life. God calls us blessed and promises us riches in heaven that last forever.

✧ We are not saved by the good things we do but because of the faith we have in Jesus who died for us.

Follow-up Activities

❀ Pick a job around the house you hate to do and throughout May serve your family by doing that job.

❀ Invite a friend over to play and serve your friend by letting him or her choose the activity you do together.

❀ Reach out into the community. Clean a park and leave paper towels or toilet paper in a bathroom that is without them.

❀ Gather some nicer used toys and clothing and donate them to a charity.

❀ Write a letter to Jesus thanking Him for forgiving your sins and remembering only the good deeds you do out of faith.

Our Response to God's Grace

Dear Jesus, King,

Help us to serve You in love by serving others, just as You served us in love by dying on the cross. In Your precious name we pray. Amen.

Ponderings

❧ In the parable in today's reading, the King separates the people into two groups—those who have served Him by serving others and those who have not served Him. To serve someone means to make that person your master. In this parable, Jesus divides those who have made Him their Master from those who have not.

❧ Is Jesus the Master of your life? How does this show?

❧ Make a practice of seeing the face of Jesus in every person with whom you come into contact. What difference will that make in how you treat people?

❧ On Judgment Day, Jesus will "bury all our failures in forgiving silence and remember only our deeds of mercy" (text note for *Concordia Self-Study Bible,* Concordia Publishing House, 1986). How blessed we are indeed to have such a loving and forgiving God!

✒ Read Matthew 25:14–30. In this parable, God blesses us with earthly gifts. On the Last Day, those who have used their gifts to serve God well will hear the beautiful words "Well done, good and faithful servant!"

✒ God's faithful have the promise of eternal blessings in the following words: "Come and share your master's happiness!" (Matthew 25:23b). "Come, you who are blessed by My Father; take your inheritance, the kingdom prepared for you since the creation of the world" (Matthew 25:34b). "People will come from east and west and north and south, and will take their places at the feast in the kingdom of God" (Luke 13:29). These promises, sealed on the cross, are an inspiration to serve our Master, our Benefactor and Lord, with love and joy!

Journal Jottings

Lilies and Birds

God's Grace to Us

Today's Reading: Matthew 6:25–34

"Look at the birds in the air; they do not sow or reap or store away in barns, and yet your heavenly Father feeds them. Are you not much more valuable than they?" Matthew 6:26

Faith Walk

Walk through a park with flowerbeds or a botanical garden. Keep your eyes open for wildlife, especially birds. Look for the most beautiful flower you can find.

Faith Talk

✧ How does God take care of birds, animals, and flowers?

✧ God loves His creation and His people, but which is of the most value to Him?

✧ What does it mean to worry? In what ways do you worry?

✧ Read the whole passage. Why shouldn't we worry?

✧ How has God taken care of you?

Follow-up Activities

❦ Make a bird feeder:

1. Tie a string to a pinecone.

2. Spread peanut butter onto a pinecone.

3. Roll the pinecone in birdseed.

4. Hang your bird feeder from a tree as a snack for birds.

✤ Do an experiment with flowers:

   1. Place a cut flower in a vase of water. Place another in a vase without water.

   2. Put two plotted flowers in a window. Water one and not the other.

   3. Place a third potted flower in a closet, close the door and ignore it.

   4. Take pictures of the different flowers daily and keep a journal of how each one develops. In two weeks, write a summary of your experiment. How does God take care of flowers?

✤ Visit a humane society and learn what it takes to care for a pet. How does God care for us?

✤ Cut pictures from magazines and make a collage of the ways God takes care of you.

✤ Make a list of all the ways you worry. Tear up the list and throw it away as a symbol of your trust in God's care for you. We have no need to worry.

Our Response to God's Grace

Dear God, Loving Father,

   Help us to give our worries to You in faith and trust, knowing that You are in control and that You love us. We pray in the name of Jesus, who nailed our worries to the cross. Amen.

Ponderings

🌀 A current buzzword is "proactive." Proactive means we can assess a situation and do something positive to shape it instead of waiting to react. According to the Scripture reading, who truly is in charge of every situation in our lives? Is this a good thing? Why? How does that make you feel?

🌀 Although God is in control, He does not leave us without the ability to reason and to act. With God's help, what is the most "proactive" thing we can do? Hint: Reread Matthew 6:33.

❧ Although we trust in God's provision, He does not remove every hardship from us. Read Hebrews 12:1–13, James 1:12, and Romans 8:28–39 for insight into God's role in our suffering. Using these verses, list God's promises in our trials and the blessings we receive through suffering.

❧ Pray for each of your worries and visualize giving them over to God. Thank God, in advance, for abundantly providing for all your needs and showering His rich blessings on you.

❧ Verse two of John Newton's hymn, "Come, My Soul, with Every Care," says:
You are coming to your King
Large petitions with you bring;
For His grace and power are such
None can ever ask too much.

❧ When we have needs, God wants us not to worry but to come to Him in prayer. Read Matthew 7:7–11. God is our loving Father and no worry, no need, no petition is too small or too large to bring to Him in prayer.

Journal Jottings

Mom's Choice!

God's Grace to Us

Today's Reading: Proverbs 31:10–31

Her children arise and call her blessed; her husband also, and he praises her. Proverbs 31:28

Faith Walk

Mom's choice! Take a walk at a favorite park, by the lake, through a mall, or in the woods—Mom's wish is your command!

Faith Talk

✧ Moms are a gift from the Lord. Read the whole Scripture selection. How has your mom been a gift?

✧ In the Bible, God commands us to honor our mothers. How can you honor your mother?

✧ Proverbs 31 describes the perfect wife and mother. It is impossible for a human mother to live up to this image. But we are to love our mothers even when they fail us. This is the greatest way to honor them, for God's forgiveness belongs to our mothers just as it belongs to us.

✧ How do mothers help us to grow in our faith and in life?

✧ What are the roles of a mother? How is God like a mother? Read Isaiah 66:13.

Follow-up Activities

❧ Create Mother's Day cards. Use a computer, paint, stamps, or stickers. Be creative!

❧ Write a letter to your mother telling her how and why you love her.

❧ Give Mom breakfast in bed, have a picnic for lunch, and take her out to eat for dinner. No cooking for Mom all day! Yeah! (Be sure to clean up the breakfast mess and picnic makings.)

❧ Make Mom a book of coupons redeemable for backrubs, chores, hugs, and the biggest slice of pie.

❧ Mom is queen for the day. Tell her she looks beautiful, let her soak in the bathtub, and give her a massage.

Our Response to God's Grace

Dear Father in Heaven,

You are the creator of all mothers. Thank You for giving me my mother and the blessings I have received through her. Help me, in turn, to be a blessing to her as I follow Your command to honor my mother. In Jesus' name. Amen.

Ponderings

✍ Write definitions of "mother" and "wife." What has shaped your image and expectations of these roles? How have these definitions influenced your life? Do you have a godly relationship with these roles, a relationship shaped by love, forgiveness, and grace? Pray that in your life "mother" and "wife" might be shaped by these characteristics.

✍ What has your relationship with your own mother been like? How has that influenced your relationship with God? With your family? Has it influenced your relationships positively or negatively? If it has been a negative influence on your relationships, what can you change to make a difference?

✍ No relationship can be intimate and whole without God's grace flowing, like a river of love, into the hearts and actions of people. Pray that God's "river of love" called grace may flow into your relationships and turn hate into love, pain into joy, and bitterness into forgiveness.

✍ If your "mother" and "wife" relationships have been ones of love, grace, and forgiveness, spend time in prayer thanking the Lord for these blessings.

❧ If your "mother" and "wife" relationships have been filled with pain, bitterness, hatred, or unforgiveness, lay these feelings at the feet of your Heavenly Father, seeking His healing touch. Ask that He guide you, forgive you, and help you to forgive yourself and others. Ask also that He shape the hearts and actions of those with whom you have a broken relationship. Finally, ask that He heal your pain in relationships that cannot be healed. Remember God has enough Mother and Father love for you to soothe even the greatest heartache. Blessed Mother's Day!

Journal Jottings

Creation Chorus

God's Grace to Us

Today's Reading: Psalm 145

Let every creature praise His holy name forever and ever. Psalm 145:21b

Faith Walk

Take a walk in an area known for an abundance of wildlife. Watch for signs of wildlife. Stop and observe one or more animals. Keep a list of everything you observe.

Faith Talk

✧ What wonderful observations about animals did you make on your walk?

✧ A bushy tailed squirrel scampering in the trees, a deer sipping water at a creek, and a bird pulling up a worm, all praise God by simply being. They speak of the power and creativity of God, the Maker and Ruler of all creation.

✧ How did the animals you observed on your walk praise God? All creatures and all of God's creation are a chorus of praise to God.

✧ How can you praise God?

Follow-up Activities

❧ Write poems about different animals. End each poem with the words "Praise the Lord!" Use these poems in family worship.

❧ Paint pictures of animals.

❧ Make a puppet show. Have each family member create an animal puppet from a paper bag and write an essay explaining how that animal praises God. For the puppet show, have the puppets take turns presenting their essay. To add fun, have the puppets act out parts of their essays.

❧ We also praise God. Have a family talent show. Invite relatives and friends to watch it and dedicate it "in praise of God."

❧ Take pictures of a variety of animals and create a photo essay of animals praising God by simply "being."

Our Response to God's Grace

Dear Father, Almighty Creator,

Zebras, fish, elephants, worms, ladybugs, butterflies, and all animals praise You for Your glorious creation. I also sing out my praise to You, O Lord. In Jesus' name. Amen.

Ponderings

☙ Find a time alone to observe an animal. What can you learn about the nature of God through His animal creation?

☙ In the Bible, animals are often used to describe the nature of God. Look up the following passages and write what each passage tells us about God.

Leviticus 17:11 and Luke 22:20
Deuteronomy 32:11 and Isaiah 40:31
Psalm 91:4 and Matthew 23:37
Psalm 23
Revelation 19:11–16
1 Peter 1:18–19
Revelation 5:5
Matthew 11:28–30

☙ Psalm 145 teaches us several things about praising God. It teaches us *who* praises God—every creature.

☙ Psalm 145 teaches us *how* to praise God. Read through the psalm. Write down every way God is praised.

☙ Psalm 145 teaches us *why* we praise God. Read through the psalm one more time. This time write the reasons the psalmist gives for praising the Lord. When you are done, write your own psalm praising the Lord.

Journal Jottings

Seed and Sock

God's Grace to Us

Today's Reading: Matthew 13:3–9 and 18–23

[Jesus said,] "But the one who received the seed that fell on the good soil is the man who hears the Word and understands it. He produces a crop yielding a hundred, sixty, or thirty times what was sown." Matthew 13:23

Faith Walk

Put on two pairs of socks—the second pair should be older socks. Walk to a park and take off your shoes. Walk around for several minutes. Take off the top pair of socks, put your shoes on and walk home. At home, dampen each dirty sock with water, place them in individual zipper bags, cut triangles in the bottom of the bags, and set them in a sunny window. Over the next week, observe the zipper bags and discover what happens to them.

Faith Talk

✧ Read the whole scripture reading. How are some people like the seed sown on the path?

✧ Why does the seed sown among rocks spring up quickly and then die? How are some people like that?

✧ How are some people like the seeds sown among thorns?

✧ How can you be like a seed sown on good soil? Hint: Read John 15:5.

✧ What crop will you produce?

Follow-up Activities

✤ Throw some seeds outside on the lawn. Over the next several days observe what happens.

✤ Go on a weed hunt in your yard or in a park. How are some people spiritually like weeds? Ask God to plant a strong faith in their hearts.

✤ Visit different areas in your community and bring home samples of the soil. Plant seeds in the different soils. As you tend and water them, determine which soil is the best for the seeds. What makes good soil for Christians to grow in their faith?

✤ Cut out heart shapes and glue seeds to them as a reminder that God plants the seeds of faith in our hearts.

✤ Give a potted plant to a friend, neighbor, or relative with some favorite Bible verses attached.

Our Response to God's Grace

Dear God, Holy Spirit,

Prepare in our hearts good soil so when the seed of Your Word is planted, our faith may grow. Please help us to plant Your Word into the soil of other people's hearts as we share the Good News of Jesus with them. In His name. Amen.

Ponderings

✐ What kind of soil has your heart been like? Write a description of how your faith has grown through your life.

✐ The environment can change soil. Over-farming the land, drought, wind, rain, fertilizer, and compost all affect the quality of soil for growing plants. In the same manner, the soil of a person's heart can be affected by life experiences. Family relationships, the death of a child, violent crime, the unexpected kindness of a stranger can all impact a person's openness to God's Word. What conditions in your life have worked in the soil of your heart?

🖝 Daily, for a week, pray that the Lord prepare in your heart a fertile soil for your faith to grow and develop.

🖝 Pray also that your children's hearts may be fertile soil and that their faith may grow strong.

🖝 How can you help prepare the soil in the hearts of those around you so they may be more open to God's Word?

Journal Jottings

To Heaven and Back

God's Grace to Us

Today's Readings: Matthew 28:16–20 and Acts 1:1–11

After He said this, He was taken up before their very eyes, and a cloud hid Him from their sight. Acts 1:9

Faith Walk

Take a walk to a park on a day when there are white, fluffy clouds in the sky. Bring an old blanket along to lay on and look up at the sky. What do the shapes of the clouds look like? Imagine what it was like to be a disciple watching Jesus ascend into heaven and disappear behind a cloud.

Faith Talk

✧ Jesus ascended (went up) to heaven to prepare a place for us. In the same manner, He will return someday to gather all believers and take them to heaven with Him.

✧ Although Jesus is physically gone from us, His Spirit remains in this world. Read Matthew 28:20b.

✧ Read 28:19–20a. How can you carry out Christ's command in these verses?

✧ Preaching God's Word to all nations seems like an impossible job, but God does not expect us to do this job alone—God's Spirit speaks through us.

Follow-up Activities

❦ Make a snack of "Cloud Puffs":

    1. Spread melted butter to within ¼" of the edge of refrigerator crescent roll "triangles."

2. Mix ⅓ c. of sugar with 1 tsp. cinnamon and sprinkle on the triangles.

3. Place one large marshmallow on each triangle and wrap the dough around the marshmallow, pinching the edges together to seal.

4. Bake at 350 degrees for 6–8 minutes or until the marshmallow begins to slightly seep out.

5. Enjoy as an ascension snack!

❧ On your home altar, create a "vision" display to remind you to watch for Jesus' return. This display should be made up of items that help people see: glasses, binoculars, a telescope, or a sun visor.

❧ Make hanging doves:

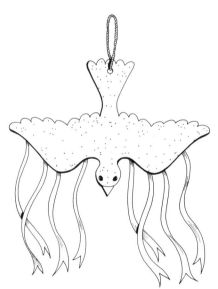

1. Cut doves (see pattern in Appendix B) from poster board.

2. Decorate them with silver glitter.

3. Attach several strands of thin white ribbon to the wings.

4. Punch a small hole in the tails. Tie a circle of ribbon through them.

5. Hang your doves in visible spots as a reminder that God's Spirit is always with us.

❧ Take a world map to church and ask your pastor to help you locate the missions your church supports. Mark these locations on your map and hang it near your home altar. Commit to praying daily for these missions.

❧ Invite an unchurched friend to a church event. Keep that person in your prayers, asking God's Spirit to create faith in your friend's heart.

Our Response to God's Grace

Dear Christ, Ascended and Present Lord,

Although Your body has ascended into heaven, Your Spirit is always with us. We know that You have gone to heaven to prepare a place for us. While we joyfully await Your return, help us witness Your love to others. For Your sake. Amen.

Ponderings

> He left them. Jesus ascended into heaven and left His disciples. He left them standing gape-mouthed and shocked. He left them staring at the clouds and awed by what had happened. He left them joyful and worshipping. Jesus left them ... but not alone. For although He was gone in the flesh, He left them with a promise—a promise to send His Spirit. His flesh was gone, but not His presence.

> He left them. Jesus left His disciples for glory—for His glory, for their glory, and for our glory. He left them to take His place at the right hand of His Father and to prepare a heavenly place for us.

> He left them. Jesus left His disciples with a promise and a hope: a promise and a hope that He extends also to us—a promise and a hope of the return of His physical presence and eternal life with Him.

> He left them. When Jesus left, His disciples were standing, but He did not leave them standing still. He left them busy. He left them busy with a job, a mission, and a commission. He left them, and us, to "go and make disciples." He left them so others may be brought to Him.

> He left them. Jesus left His disciples, and us—rich in His presence, His promises, and His Spirit!

Journal Jottings

June

june

A Church for All Nations

God's Grace to Us

Today's Reading: Acts 2:1–42

All of them were filled with the Holy Spirit and began to speak in other tongues as the Spirit enabled them. Acts 2:4

Faith Walk

Take a walk around a place filled with many different people, for example a monument, mall, or airport. Are there people of different nationalities? Do you hear people speaking in different languages?

Faith Talk

✧ Jesus kept His promise and on Pentecost sent His Holy Spirit to the believers.

✧ The Spirit came in a violent wind that filled the house. Wind or breath is a symbol of God's Spirit.

✧ Tongues of fire rested on the heads of each of the believers. The fire pointed ahead to the disciples' speaking in tongues. Fire is a symbol of God's presence and power.

✧ The disciples spoke the Good News of Jesus' resurrection to the people of many nations who were gathered in Jerusalem. (People from many nations were gathered in this one place to celebrate the harvest.) The Spirit helped them speak in languages they had never learned.

✧ Three thousand people received God's Spirit, were baptized, and became followers of Christ on Pentecost. God equips us also to tell others the Good News that Jesus is alive. Through Baptism, His Spirit brings them to faith. How can you tell others about this wonderful Good News?

Follow-up Activities

✤ At night light some candles in your home, turn off all the lights, and silently imagine what it was like to be a disciple when the Spirit came to them on Pentecost. Share your insights with one another.

✤ Celebrate Pentecost. Decorate a cake with candles. Light the candles and blow them out. The burning candles remind us that God came to the disciples. You blew out the candles; God blew in His Spirit.

✤ Make windsocks:

1. For each windsock, decorate a white paper bag with markers.

2. Write a slogan, such as "Spirit wind" or "Tongues of fire," on the bag to remind you of Pentecost.

3. Add streamers to the opening of the bag.

4. Tape a looped string to the bottom of the bag and hang outside on a windy (but dry!) day.

✤ Put a pan of water and some shells on your home altar as a reminder of the gift of Baptism.

✤ Practice witnessing by telling your family about Jesus' resurrection.

Our Response to God's Grace

Dear Holy Spirit,

Thank You for coming to the disciples on Pentecost so all people might know about Jesus. Thank You also for coming into our own hearts at Baptism. Give us the words to tell others about Jesus. In His name. Amen.

Ponderings

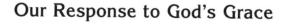 Imagine the joy the disciples felt when they were filled with the Spirit on Pentecost. Jesus had kept His promise to send His Spirit. This was evidence

that Jesus was still among them and that at His ascension He had not left them alone.

❧ Pentecost transformed the disciples. They went from a ragged group of men who deserted and denied Jesus at the cross to a group of 3,000-plus believers made bold by the Spirit.

❧ The Spirit came to the disciples in wind and fire and to the new believers in the water and the Word.

❧ How did God come to His people in the following Bible verses?

Ezekiel 37:9–10 and 14
John 3:8
Exodus 3:2
John 1:14
Matthew 28:19

❧ How did God come to you? Write your story. How can you help God come to others?

Journal Jottings

Water Way

God's Grace to Us

Today's Reading: Acts 2:37–47

Peter replied, "Repent and be baptized, every one of you, in the name of Jesus Christ for the forgiveness of your sins. And you will receive the gift of the Holy Spirit. This promise is for you and your children and for all who are far off— for all whom the Lord our God will call." Acts 2:38–39

Faith Walk

Walk around or near a body of water such as a lake or river. Is the water moving or is it calm?

Faith Talk

✧ Imagine being a part of the crowd listening to Peter speak on Pentecost, watching as 3,000 people were baptized into the Christian church, and then coming forward and feeling the water upon your head as the Holy Spirit entered your heart. Describe what you think it would have been like. Read Acts 2:38–39 and Titus 3:3–7.

✧ What does it mean to repent? How is repentance a part of our daily life?

✧ What gifts does God promise us through Baptism?

✧ Through the forgiveness we receive in Baptism, we are made clean in the eyes of God. No longer do our sins stand in the way of a relationship with God. We receive this forgiveness because Jesus died on the cross to take the punishment for our sins.

✧ Reread verses 42–47. As we are baptized, the Holy Spirit enters our hearts. How does the Holy Spirit's presence and power change our hearts and lives?

Follow-up Activities

✤ At your Baptism you were born again into Christ's family. Celebrate your Baptism birthdays. Light a candle to represent the Light of Christ piercing the darkness of your hearts as you received God's forgiveness in Baptism. Have a "birthday cake" with candles. Sing "Happy Baptism Birthday" (melody: "Happy Birthday to You") or a baptism hymn.

✤ Receive daily baptismal forgiveness. Make a family habit of confessing your sins to one another at dinnertime, devotions, or bedtime. Remind one another of the forgiveness we receive through Baptism.

✤ Make Baptism magnets:

1. Cut out cardboard hearts (see pattern in Appendix B).

2. Paint the hearts red with tempera paint.

3. After the paint dries, paint three blue water drops on each heart.

4. Add magnets to the backs and hang on the refrigerator as a reminder that God's Spirit comes into our hearts at Baptism.

✤ Reread verses 42–47 of the Bible passage. Choose one way your family can better live "in the Spirit." Ask God daily to help you live in His Spirit.

✤ Celebrate the blessings of God's Water and Word in your life with a family swimming party.

Our Response to God's Grace

Dear Father in heaven,

Thank You for giving us the blessings of Your forgiveness through the water and the Word coming together in Baptism. Give us the power, through Your Spirit, to live for You each day. Through Your Son. Amen.

Ponderings

🖋 A spiritual transformation is described in several accounts in Scripture. The people are confronted with their sin and feel their guilt. They repent and are baptized into faith in Christ. At Baptism, the Holy Spirit enters their hearts and they become reflections of Christ. Forgiveness is ours through Baptism, and we are declared righteous because of justification, which is being made right in God's eyes because Christ took our sins to the cross. The work of the Holy Spirit in our hearts is called "sanctification," which is a renewal of our whole life, whereby we become more Christ-like in our thoughts, words, and actions. What does God's work of justification and sanctification mean in your life?

🖋 Baptism is a means by which we receive God's grace and are brought into His kingdom. In Baptism, we are saved from sin. Read 1 Peter 3:18–22. Rewrite this passage and its meaning in your own words.

🖋 Read Exodus 13:17–14:31. How is this story an image of Baptism?

🖋 Use Ezekiel 36:25–30 as a basis for meditating on the meaning, purpose, and blessings of Baptism.

🖋 How is the Christian community in Acts 2:42–47 a mission statement for the whole church of God? How can your family better reflect that mission?

Journal Jottings

Flag Find

God's Grace to Us

Today's Reading: Matthew 5:13–16

[Jesus said,] "In the same way, let your light shine before men, that they may see your good deeds and praise your Father in heaven." Matthew 5:16

Faith Walk

As you take a walk in your community, count the flags you see. What other signs or symbols, such as a stop sign, can you find?

Faith Talk

✧ What is the purpose of a sign or a symbol?

✧ What does the flag symbolize?

✧ What are some of the signs and symbols of the Christian faith?

✧ How can you be a living sign of faith, a light to the world?

✧ Why should we live as lights to the world?

Follow-up Activities

❉ Make individual and family flags, using waterproof fabric (can be found in a fabric store), that represent your faith. Be creative! Hot glue the flags to a dowel or wooden rod. Take turns hanging the flags outside as a witness of your faith.

❉ Choose one night to leave your porch light on from sunset to sunrise as reminder that our lights are to be shining in the world as a sign of your faith in Christ.

♣ Make homemade beeswax candles. (Foundation beeswax sheets and wick or natural fiber string can be found in discount and hobby stores.)

1. Warm the beeswax sheets in the sun until slightly floppy.

2. Cut wick or string one centimeter longer than the candles. Press the wick along one edge of the beeswax sheet.

3. Starting at the wick edge, roll the sheet tightly and firmly to form the body of the candle.

4. Place in a candleholder and light! (An adult should light the candle.)

♣ Write a list of uses for salt. Why does Jesus call us the salt of the earth?

♣ Paint paper plates blue and green to symbolize the earth. Before the paint dries, sprinkle salt over the plates. After the paint dries, hang the plates in a prominent location as a reminder that we are the salt of the earth.

♣ Be salt and light to people with weak faith or no faith. Have each family member choose someone who needs a spiritual light. Ask God to help you be a light to that person. Commit to praying for and encouraging that person. Go out of your way to show love to him or her. Ask God for opportunities to share the Gospel with the person you have chosen.

Our Response to God's Grace

Dear Father, Giver of Grace,

Help us to share the message of Your grace to the world.

Dear Jesus, Lord of Light,

Help us to be lights to the world.

Dear Spirit, Source of Truth,

Help us to be the salt of the earth. For the sake of Jesus Christ, the Light that shines in the darkness. Amen.

Ponderings

☞ One of the uses for salt in biblical times was to preserve food. How are we, as the salt of the earth, used by God to preserve the faith?

☞ Another use for salt was to add flavoring. How do we "flavor" the world?

☞ What is our relationship to the light of the world and the Light of Christ? To answer this question, reread verses 14–16 of the Scripture reading. Read also:

John 1:1–14
John 3:19–21
John 8:12
John 12:35–36
Philippians 2:14–16

☞ Use the following selections from Psalms to write a description of God as the Light:

Psalm 27:1
Psalm 36:9
Psalm 76:4
Psalm 104:1–2
Psalm 119:105
Psalm 139

☞ Spend some time in darkness, meditating on the light of Christ shining into a world dark with sin. To help with your meditation, memorize Isaiah 60:1.

Journal Jottings

Dad's the Boss!

God's Grace to Us

Today's Reading: Proverbs 23:15–25

Listen to your Father, who gave you life. Proverbs 23:22a

Faith Walk

Dad's choice! Go on a walk around a golf course (with clubs and balls, of course!), at a lake (with fishing poles), or hiking at a state park. Dad's the boss!

Faith Talk

✧ Dads are a gift of the Lord. How has your dad been a gift?

✧ Your dad has given you the precious gift of life.

✧ Read the whole Scripture selection. What is the greatest gift that a child can give a father? Why?

✧ The most important role of a father is to raise his children in the faith and train them in righteous living. That is a Christian father's joy and delight. Why? How does your father teach you the faith and train you in righteous living?

✧ How is God your Father? Read Romans 8:12–17.

Follow-up Activities

❦ Use sidewalk chalk to make a Father's Day "card" on your sidewalk and let the world know what a wonderful Dad you have.

❦ Write a letter telling Dad you love him and why. Tell him some of things he has taught you.

❦ Choose an extra chore to help Dad with this week.

❧ Do something special with Dad. Go see a sporting event. Take a bike ride somewhere. Watch his favorite television program with him. Or eat out at Dad's favorite restaurant.

❧ Pray for Dad, asking God to help him in his role as your spiritual teacher.

Our Response to God's Grace

Dear Abba Father,

Thank You for our dads here on earth and for being our perfect Father in heaven. Help my dad to be a strong spiritual leader and man. Help us to please Dad and to glorify You with our words, actions, and faith. In the name of Your Son, Jesus. Amen.

Ponderings

❧ Define "Father," "Dad," and "Husband." Have the real "fathers," "dads," and "husbands" in your life lived up to these definitions? How has that shaped your relationship to them? To God?

❧ The Bible tells us that God is our Father. But if we have a bad relationship with our earthly father, it becomes difficult to have a godly father-child relationship with our heavenly Father.

❧ How can we trust that our heavenly Father is loving if our earthly dad has not been loving? How can we understand His forgiveness if our dad has been unforgiving? How can we feel accepted if our dad has been critical? For many people, their relationship with their own fathers has been a roadblock to faith. If you, or anyone you know, is struggling with this difficulty, pray that the Holy Spirit bring His healing balm to the relationship. When relationships cannot be healed because of hardness of heart or death, ask that the Holy Spirit help those who are hurting to move past that relationship and to embrace the perfect father-child relationship found in the heavenly Father.

❧ If your relationship with your dad has been loving and warm, spend time in prayer thanking the Lord for that blessing.

✐ Use the following verses to define God as the heavenly Father:
   2 Samuel 7:11b–14
   Psalm 68:5–6
   Psalm 103:13
   Romans 8:1–17

✐ Describe a relationship of perfect intimacy and love with our heavenly Father. Write this description down.

Journal Jottings

Celebrate Summer

God's Grace to Us

Today's Reading: Psalm 96

Let the fields be jubilant, and everything in them. Then all the trees of the forest will sing for joy. Psalm 96:12

Faith Walk

On the first day of summer, take a walk on a nature path and look for ways summer is bursting forth in joy.

Faith Talk

✧ What is your favorite season? Why?

✧ What is your favorite thing about summer?

✧ How does summer sing of God's splendor?

✧ What wonderful things about God's creation can you discover and learn?

✧ Stop, look, and listen to summer. What does it seem to be saying to you about God?

Follow-up Activities

❧ Have a "Celebrate Summer" party. Invite some friends over and stay outside until the sky is full of stars. Barbecue hamburgers and hot dogs for supper and roast marshmallows for dessert.

❧ Play your favorite yard games. End the evening with a prayer under the stars, thanking God for summer.

❧ Make a nature collage. Collect nature items such as leaves, twigs, and pebbles, and glue them to a piece of cardboard.

❧ Write a family book of poems praising God for nature.

❧ Check out books from the library on nature and learn more about God's creation.

❧ Have fun climbing trees. Celebrate summer!

Our Response to God's Grace

Dear Heavenly Father, God of all Nature,

We praise You for the gift of Your creation. Help us to see You and Your majesty reflected in it. Through the glory of Jesus. Amen.

Ponderings

✐ Reconnect with God's creation. Write a journal entry on nature.

✐ Reconnect with God's creation. Read Psalms 104 and 148.

✐ Reconnect with God's creation. Spend quiet time alone outside, meditating on the Creator and His creation. Praise God for His creation.

✐ Reconnect with God's creation. Even if you are not an artist, paint, draw, or make a craft reflecting God's creation.

✐ Reconnect with God's creation. Plan a family weekend at a nature area. As you do, reflect on the majesty of God's creation and the majesty of God the creator.

Journal Jottings

Colors in Nature

God's Grace to Us

Today's Reading: Genesis 2:8–14 and 19–20a

Now the Lord God had planted a garden in the east, in Eden; and there He put the man He had formed. Genesis 2:8

Faith Walk

Walk through a nature area or park. As you do, open your eyes and look for the many colors in nature.

Faith Talk

✧ Close your eyes and imagine the Garden of Eden. Look at the plants and animals, the flowers and birds. What do you see in your mind's eye? Describe it.

✧ Immediately following creation, none of the animals had yet gone extinct. They were all there in the garden. In the same garden were the largest dinosaur and the smallest flea. In the garden were the colorful parrot and the plain gray mouse, the round elephant and the skinny centipede. Every color, shape, and form imaginable in the animal kingdom was in the garden.

✧ In the Garden of Eden was every plant, flower, tree, and shrub that God had created. Reds, blues, yellows, blacks—every color was represented. Spiked flowers and rounded leaves, tall grasses and flat moss were all together in God's garden.

✧ Many plants and animals are now extinct. We do not know if the dinosaurs were green, brown, or even florescent blue. Think about the plants and animals that existed in the Garden of Eden that today are beyond even our imagination!

✧ We may not be able to see the vivid beauty of the garden God first created, but we can look around and see the sunflowers bursting forth in yellow, the green of the hummingbird, and the bright orange of the monarch butterfly—and we can give praise to God, the Master Painter.

Follow-up Activities

❧ Explore God's colorful world further by visiting an aquarium or the fish section of a pet store. What colors do you see?

❧ Take a field trip to a botanical garden or a nature preserve. What colors do you see?

❧ Go to a zoo and make a list of all the animals. What colors do you see?

❧ Start a scrapbook titled "The Color of God's World." Take photos, color pictures, or purchase postcards to add to your scrapbook. What colors do you see?

❧ Check out a nature video from the library or a video store, or watch a nature program on television. What colors do you see? Praise God for colors!

Our Response to God's Grace

Dear Father, Creator and Master Artist,

We hold in awe the beauty, creativity, colors, and forms You used in designing the world. We praise You for Your wonderful work, O God! With You we say, "It is good!" In Jesus' name. Amen.

Ponderings

✎ Take time to ponder the gift of color. Has the black hair of a newborn baby or the graying hair of a grandparent had an impact on you? Has the rainbow reflections of a diamond or the black of a funeral procession touched your heart? How has God used color to speak to your spirit? How do these reflections bring you back to what you have learned about God in His Word?

✎ Ponder the color gray—the color of ashes. Read Job 42:6. What is the significance of "gray"?

- Ponder the color red. Read Isaiah 1:18 and John 19:34. What is the significance of "red"?

- Ponder the color white. Read Psalm 51 and Revelation 7:13–17. What is the significance of "white"?

- Ponder the colors in your church. Do you see the brown of the pews? It can remind you of the brown on Christ's cross. Do you see the red in the eternal flame? It can remind you of the red of Christ's blood.

- Ask your pastor to explain the significance of the colors used for different seasons or festivals in your church. What color is used for Christmas, Lent, Good Friday, Pentecost?

Journal Jottings

July

Let Freedom Ring

God's Grace to Us

Today's Reading: Romans 6:15–23

But now that you have been set free from sin and have become slaves to God, the benefit you reap leads to holiness, and the result is eternal life. Romans 6:22

Faith Walk

Go on a neighborhood hunt looking for signs of Independence Day.

Faith Talk

✧ Retell the story of Independence Day.

✧ What does freedom mean?

✧ How has Jesus set us free?

✧ With freedom comes responsibility. What responsibilities do we have in our country? What responsibilities do we have as citizens of God's kingdom? What blessings do we have?

✧ Let freedom ring. How can we celebrate the freedom of our country and the freedom we have through Jesus?

Follow-up Activities

❦ Make an Independence Day cake:

1. Frost a cake with white icing.

2. In the upper left-hand corner add a blue background with blueberries.

3. Use strawberries for red stripes.

♣ Braid red, white, and blue pieces of embroidery floss or narrow ribbon and tie the ends together to make a freedom bracelet. This bracelet is to be a reminder that God has blessed us with two kinds of freedom—we live in a free country and through Jesus we are free from the slavery of sin.

♣ Read the newspaper and clip out examples of our freedom and ways freedom is used properly or abused. Discuss the newspaper clippings.

♣ Write a letter to the editor of your local newspaper addressing freedom and responsibility.

♣ Write a "Declaration of Independence from Sin" and a "Bill of Rights and Responsibilities for Citizens of the Kingdom of God."

Our Response to God's Grace

Dear Triune God, Giver of Freedom,

Thank You for the blessings of freedom You have given us, both in our nation and in the kingdom of God. Help us to be responsible citizens, bringing glory and honor to You, our King. Through the freedom that is ours in Christ. Amen.

Ponderings

☞ How has sin held you bondage in your life?

☞ What does it mean to be "slaves to God" or "slaves to righteousness"?

☞ Read Romans 8 for a picture of what it means to be free from sin and slaves to righteousness.

☞ God, by the blood of His Son, has made us heirs of His kingdom and free from the slavery of sin. The kingdom of heaven is not a democracy, but a theocracy. How does that define our relationship to God? Does it make us less free? How? Why?

☞ Much of the world is not free. In Saudi Arabia, women are murdered for being abused by men. In China, Christians are persecuted. In Korea, mass graves are filled with the bodies of people who were "too educated." In America,

God has gifted us with freedom. People can worship the god of their choice, speak their minds, go into any law-abiding profession they choose, and pursue happiness. But we, as Americans, often take our rights for granted. What a dangerous attitude! Apathy can lead to the slippery slope of loss, the loss of our freedoms. We have the responsibility to protect our freedoms through practicing our religion, voicing our opinions, participating in our political process, and guarding our freedoms. Evaluate yourself. Have you been careful to exercise and protect your freedom? In what ways can you do a better job? Thank the Lord for the freedoms He has given you and ask Him for wisdom in using them righteously.

Journal Jottings

Family Parade Entry

God's Grace to Us

Today's Reading: Acts 5:17–25

"Go, stand in the temple courts," [the angel] said, "and tell the people the full message of this new life." Acts 5:20

Faith Walk

Put together a family float proclaiming the message of the freedom found in Jesus and enter it in a local Independence Day parade.

Faith Talk

✧ True freedom comes only through faith in Christ. Through Him we are free from sin, death, and the power of Satan!

✧ We have an exciting message to spread to the world! Christ has won the war for freedom! People who do not receive this message or do not understand it will die still enslaved by sin. Like the apostles, we must do everything we can to spread this Gospel message!

✧ Spreading the Gospel message is sometimes a difficult task, but we are not alone in this job. In the same way God opened the prison doors for the apostles so they could continue to preach the news, He opens our mouths and gives us the words to speak so others may learn.

Follow-up Activities

❧ Design a family shield (see Appendix B for a pattern) that proclaims the freedom found in Jesus.

❧ If you have Internet access and have web space, create a web page proclaiming victory through Jesus.

✤ Prior to Independence Day, place Christian tracts in the restrooms of public picnic facilities.

✤ Using fabric paint, create individual t-shirts witnessing Christ crucified.

✤ Hand out Christian stickers, fortune cookies, or bookmarks at Independence Day festivities.

Our Response to God's Grace

Dear Father, Lord of Freedom,

Give us boldness to spread Your message to the whole world so others may receive the freedom found in You. In the name of the crucified Christ. Amen.

Ponderings

✐ Read the remainder of Acts chapter five (verses 26–42). How does the experience of the apostles apply to your own life?

✐ The book of Acts is filled with believers boldly proclaiming the Word of God and nonbelievers coming into a saving relationship with Jesus. Acts 4:23–31 teaches us the qualities needed to be effective witnesses:

  • Unity in spirit and mind
  • Confidence in prayer
  • Knowledge of God's Word
  • God's Spirit boldly working through His people

  How can you apply these qualities to your witnessing?

✐ Set aside a time each day to devote to praying for God's help in boldly giving witness to His love, faithfulness, and grace.

✐ Ask God for the discernment to see, with spiritual eyes, the needs of the people with whom you come into contact and to know how to minister to those needs.

✐ Bring your family to worship so you might be strengthened in your role as a spiritual army proclaiming the victory found in Christ.

Journal Jottings

Picnic Party

God's Grace to Us

Today's Reading: Exodus 12:1–30

That same night they are to eat the meat roasted over the fire, along with bitter herbs, and bread made without yeast. Exodus 12:8

Faith Walk

Walk to a picnic area. Have each family member carry one or more picnic items. Together, share a meal.

Faith Talk

✧ Throughout the Bible, God used meals to draw His children closer to Him.

✧ In the story told in today's reading, God's people had to prepare their meal hurriedly so they could quickly flee Egypt. Each part of the traditional Passover meal tells a part of this story of the flight from Egypt. For example, the bitter herbs are a reminder of the bitterness the Hebrews suffered when they were slaves in Egypt.

✧ The Passover also reminded people of the promise of the Messiah. For example, the blood of the lamb that was painted on the doorway represented the blood of the Lamb of God that was "painted" on the cross.

✧ How can your family use meals to draw closer to one another and be drawn closer to God?

Follow-up Activities

❧ Check out books on Passover from the library. Look for ones that tell how to celebrate a Christian Passover, or search for articles on the Internet. Use these books or articles as resources for celebrating your own Passover meal.

- If there is a Messianic Jewish synagogue in your community, make an appointment to visit with someone from the congregation and learn about how they celebrate Passover.
- Write a book of family mealtime prayers and make an effort to eat as many meals together as possible.
- Brainstorm a list of ways your family meals can become more faith-centered. Choose one item from the list to use in your family mealtimes.
- Passover was the last meal the Israelites ate before they were freed from the slavery of Egypt. The Lord's Supper, where Jesus gave us the bread of His body and the wine of His blood, was the last meal Jesus ate before He earned for us freedom from the slavery of sin. When we became the children of God through Baptism, we received the freedom earned for us through Jesus' death.
- Commemorate this freedom through a special family meal at the Baptism anniversaries of family members:
  1. Eat lamb as a reminder that because Jesus was the Lamb of God without blemish we could become lambs of God.
  2. Drink water as a reminder that we have received the gift of God's grace through the water of Baptism.
  3. Light a candle as a reminder that at Baptism the fire of God's Spirit entered our hearts.

Our Response to God's Grace

Dear Jesus, Bread of Life,

Each time we eat together as a family, help us recall that You gave Your body and blood to set us free from the slavery of sin. May our family meals be a time where we feast on the fellowship of Your love for us and on our love for one another. In Your saving name. Amen.

Ponderings

In Jewish tradition, meals represented fellowship. Jewish hospitality required that guests be served a meal. Agreements were sealed with meals. Weddings were celebrated with seven days of feasting. And when Jesus ate and fellowshipped with sinners, He was scorned. What kind of fellowship takes place at your family table?

❧ Are you aware of God's presence at your family table? How can you make Him a more central part of your meals?

❧ For help creating family meals of faith fellowship, consider these examples given to us in the Bible:

Mark 14:12–26
Acts 3:42
Exodus 23:14–19

❧ More important than the physical food we eat is the spiritual food of which we partake. Read John 6:25–59. How is Jesus the Bread of Life?

❧ How often do you partake of Christ's body and blood as offered at His altar for the forgiveness of your sins? Take advantage of every opportunity to come into His presence and feast on His grace.

❧ Fasting, or giving up food for a period of time, can be another way to commune with God. Read what the Bible says on this subject:

Zechariah 7:5–6
Matthew 6:16–18
Acts 13:2–3 and 14:2–3

Journal Jottings

Grains of Sand

God's Grace to Us

Today's Reading: Genesis 22:1–19

I will surely bless you and make your descendants as numerous as the stars in the sky and as the sand on the seashore. Genesis 22:17a

Faith Walk

Take a walk along a sandy shore (or find a sandbox to visit). Pick up a handful of sand and let it run through your fingers. Try counting the grains of sand you can hold in your hand. Is it possible?

Faith Talk

✧ How many grains of sand are there in the world?

✧ Why did God promise Abraham that he would be the father of a nation?

✧ Who are Abraham's descendants? Hint: Read Romans 4:16.

✧ What blessing do those who are children of Abraham receive? Read Romans 4:7–8.

✧ Reread the whole Bible passage. How does this passage remind us of Jesus?

Follow-up Activities

❦ If you know the song "Father Abraham," sing it together and do the actions.

❦ Place a cup of sand on your home altar as a reminder that we are children of Abraham.

* Lie down outside on a starry night and count the stars. Abraham's children are as numerous as the stars.

* You are a star, a child of Abraham. Cut stars from construction paper and decorate them with glitter. (See Appendix B for pattern.)

* By faith in Christ we are made righteous and become descendants of Abraham. Use your imagination to describe faith and make a poster with the theme "faith."

Our Response to God's Grace

Dear Father of Abraham, Isaac, Joseph, and me,

Thank You for giving me the gift of faith in Jesus, my Savior, so I may be a child of Abraham—Your child. In Your Son's name we pray. Amen.

Ponderings

God promised Abraham that He would make him the father of many. Abraham waited until he was an old man and finally was given a son. Then God asked Abraham to sacrifice his son to the Lord. How would you have reacted? Abraham reacted in faith. He took Isaac to the top of a mountain and prepared to sacrifice him.

Abraham lifted the knife to stab Isaac and God stopped him. God did not want Isaac's life; he wanted Abraham's faith. When Abraham, in faith, prepared to give God his only son, God credited it to him as righteousness. Abraham was made righteous not by works but by faith.

- God provided a ram for Abraham to sacrifice, a ram whose horns were caught in thorns, a perfect ram without blemish or spot.

- God gave us His Son, His only Son, a Lamb without blemish or spot but with a crown of thorns as a sacrifice for us. Because of the sacrificial offering God made for us, as we can be made righteous through faith. God wants not our works, for they are but filthy rags in His eyes. He wants our hearts.

- Read, study, and meditate on Romans 3 and 4 to better understand justification through faith—what it means to be a child of Abraham, therefore a child of God, and the impact this relationship has on our lives.

Journal Jottings

Shifting Sand

God's Grace to Us

Today's Reading: Matthew 7:24–27

[Jesus said,] "But everyone who hears these words of Mine and does not put them into practice is like a foolish man who built his house on sand." Matthew 7:26

Faith Walk

Take another walk along a sandy beach. Stay close to the shoreline. Pay close attention to what happens to the sand when the waves crash in.

Faith Talk

✧ What happens to the sand when the waves crash in?

✧ How is building a house on sand like people who do not believe in Jesus? What will happen to them?

✧ How is the faith of believers like a house built on rock?

✧ What are you built on, "sand" or "rock"? Why?

✧ How can Christ, the Rock, who is also the Word of God, build and strengthen your spirit?

Follow-up Activities

❦ Build a sand castle. Spray it with water from a hose. What happened?

❦ Spray the foundation of your house with a hose. What happened? From what material is the foundation made?

✤ Find some large flat rocks and paint the word "faith" on them using tempera paints. After the rocks dry, place them on your altar as a reminder that putting your faith in Christ is like building on a foundation of rock.

✤ Commit to memory this verse: "Trust in the Lord forever, for the Lord, the Lord, is the Rock eternal" (Isaiah 26:4). To help you memorize the passage, write it on a strip of paper and cut the words apart. Assemble it several times as a puzzle.

✤ Sing the hymn "Rock of Ages."

Our Response to God's Grace

Dear Father, Rock of Ages,

Help us to build our foundation on You, the Rock, and not on the shifting sand of the world. In the name of Jesus, our Rock. Amen.

Ponderings

✍ A thesaurus might give the following words for rock: stone, boulder, pebble, rubble, cobblestone, gravel, crag, granite, ore, and bedrock. It is the last word, bedrock, which seems to fit best with the definition of rock in this parable as found in today's reading and in Luke 6:47–49.

✍ Bedrock is a ground layer, the foundation upon which the house in the parable is built. Jesus is saying that not only is His Word a rock, it is the foundation. Many homes have rock *in* them (for example, a fireplace made of stone). But Jesus is saying He wants us to be built *on* the Rock. What is the difference between making Jesus a rock in our lives and making Him the bedrock of our lives?

✍ Sand is made of not one grain, but scores of grains. How are the values of the world like grains of sand?

✍ Wind, rain, and waves can easily change, or shift, the direction of the sand. What examples of this can you see in the values and philosophies of the world?

✍ What is the result of building our house on Christ, the Rock? Read 1 Peter 2:4–12.

❧ What has your spirit been built on? The shifting sands of the values and philosophies of the world? Or the Christ, the Living Stone? Trust in Christ to be your Rock.

Journal Jottings

Hearty Habitats

God's Grace to Us

Today's Reading: John 14:15–21

[Jesus said,] "On that day you will realize that I am in My Father, and you are in Me, and I am in you." John 14:20

Faith Walk

Take a walk in the country or a wooded area and look for evidence of possible animal habitats.

Faith Talk

✧ What is a habitat?

✧ What do plants and animals need to make a hearty, good habitat? An ideal habitat is clean, is filled with an abundance of food, provides adequate shelter, and is safe.

✧ The Bible verse says that God is in us. Our hearts are a habitat for God.

✧ Read verse 17 of the Scripture reading. What two things does it take for our hearts to be a habitat for the Spirit?

✧ Typically animals look for a place to live that is already an appropriate habitat— ready for them with maybe a few minor changes. But the Holy Spirit creates in us a place where He will dwell. Read Psalm 51:10–12.

Follow-up Activities

♣ Research animal habitats.

♣ Do something to make your yard a better habitat for animals. For example, put out an ear of corn for the squirrels, an upside-down garbage can lid with water for a birdbath, or leafy greens for rabbits.

♣ Hold your hands over your hearts and pray that God will create in you a habitat in which His Spirit dwells and pours forth richly into the world. Repeat this prayer nightly for a week.

♣ A pure habitat for the Spirit in our hearts includes obedience to God's commands, which reflects God's love dwelling in us. Have each family member choose one way in which he or she can strive to better keep God's law. Ask for God's help in doing so and for His forgiveness when you fail.

♣ We call the church "God's House." What can you do to help make your church the best habitat possible for the family of God to come into His presence?

♣ Find one item outside that reflects a plant or animal habitat and place it on your altar as a reminder that our hearts are a habitat for the Spirit.

Our Response to God's Grace

Dear Spirit of Truth,

Create in me a clean heart, a pure habitat for Your dwelling. May Your love flow through me into all the world. In Jesus' name. Amen.

Ponderings

✐ For 33 years Christ made His habitat the earth. In the Scripture reading He tells the disciples that soon He will no longer be physically present on the earth but that He will send His Spirit to dwell in the hearts of the believers. They will not see His physical presence but they will "see" Him with their heart, their spirit. Read all of John 14. How does the Spirit make His indwelling known to believers?

~ According to this chapter, what is the relationship between the Father, the Son, and the Holy Spirit?

~ What is our relationship with the Father, the Son, and the Holy Spirit?

~ In our society, when people are "fused" to one another, it is seen in a negative light. In John 15:1–17, how is fusion portrayed in a positive light?

~ Write a description of the spiritual environment that is created between believers and God as shown to us in John chapters 14 and 15.

Journal Jottings

August

Sunrise Splendor

God's Grace to Us

Today's Reading: Habakkuk 3

His splendor was like the sunrise; rays flashed from His hand, where His power was hidden. Habakkuk 3:4

Faith Walk

Take an early morning walk to the top of a hill or other spot where you can observe the sunrise.

Faith Talk

✧ Describe the sunrise. How is God like the sunrise?

✧ Read the second half of verse three. Why did Habakkuk describe God as "like the sunrise?"

✧ Use Habakkuk 3 to complete the phrases "God is ..." and "with God I am ..."

✧ How would you describe God?

Follow-up Activities

❧ Have a sunrise breakfast picnic and ponder God's presence in the sunrise. Retell the story of creation. Do you remember on which day God created the sun, moon, and stars?

❧ Write a poem comparing God to the sunrise.

❧ Paint or color a picture of a sunrise.

❧ Listen silently to the early morning birds. How is their singing like a song of praise to God?

❧ If you have a video camera, make a video titled "Images of God" and videotape a sunrise, a sunset, a rain shower, birds singing, and other nature images that reflect various attributes of God.

Our Response to God's Grace

Dear Father, God of Splendor and Might,

Like the sunrise, You burst forth in brilliance and power. You are mighty in Your saving deeds and majestic in Your power. In the name of the Risen Son. Amen.

Ponderings

↶ "His splendor was like the sunrise; rays flashed from His hand where His power was hidden" (Habakkuk 3:4). *Splendor. Sunrise. Rays. Flashed. Power. ... God is a God of might.* While at times His power may seem hidden, like the sun at night, His power is always present in our lives and will burst forth like the sunrays, covering the heavens, filling the earth, and bringing forth His glorious plan of judgment and salvation.

↶ "He stood, and shook the earth; He looked and made the nations tremble. The ancient mountains crumbled and the age-old hills collapsed. His ways are eternal" (Habakkuk 3:6). *Shook. Tremble. Crumbled. Collapsed. Eternal. ... While the world crumbles and collapses, God remains a constant and eternal strength.* He is the Alpha and the Omega, the Beginning and the End, the God of Today and the God of Eternity. And His ways are changeless.

↶ "Sun and moon stood still in the heavens in the glint of Your flying arrows, at the lightning of Your flashing spear" (Habakkuk 3:11). *Sun and moon stood still. Flying arrows. Flashing spear. ... Time stood still; God's action did not.* (See Joshua 10:12–13.) God clearly is in charge and His purposes shall be accomplished.

↶ "I heard and my heart pounded, my lips quivered at the sound; decay crept into my bones, and my legs trembled" (Habakkuk 3:16a). *Heard. Pounded. Quivered. Decay. Trembled. ... The power, strength, and might of God as He brings judgment on the wicked is so great that even hearing of it can cause us to tremble and decay.*

✐ "The Sovereign Lord is my strength; He makes my feet like the feet of a deer, He enables me to go on the heights" (Habakkuk 3:19). *Sovereign Lord. Strength. Feet of a deer. Enables. Heights. ... The God who judges the wicked and inspires fear is also the God who strengthens the righteous and enables them to rise above the storms.* Just as God brings judgment to the wicked, He also brings salvation to those who put their faith, hope, and confidence in the Risen Son. You are in God's hands.

Journal Jottings

Sunshiny Day

God's Grace to Us

Today's Reading: Isaiah 60:19–22

The sun will no more be your light by day, nor will the brightness of the moon shine on you, for the Lord will be your everlasting light, and your God will be your glory. Isaiah 60:19

Faith Walk

Take a walk on a sunny day, paying extra attention to the brightness of the outdoors.

Faith Talk

✧ Imagine the brightness of the center of the sun.

✧ How many sources of light can you name?

✧ God's brilliance is brighter than the center of the sun and all sources of light combined.

✧ In Heaven there will no longer be a sun, a moon, or stars, for God's radiance will shine light into every corner of the universe.

✧ God's radiance, His glory, will fill the land.

Follow-up Activities

❧ Make a three-dimensional sun:

1. Blow up a large round balloon.

2. Dip strips of newspaper into liquid starch and use them to cover the balloon. Let dry between layers. Keep adding newspaper strips until you have a ¼"-thick covering.

3. Leave an opening at the top of the balloon.

4. After the last layer of newspaper strips dries, pop the balloon and pull it out through the opening.

5. Paint with yellow tempera paint and add, in black, the words "God will be your glory."

❦ On a sunny day, have a hunt around your yard and look for shadowy spaces. In heaven there will be no shadows. God's glory will shine into every corner.

❦ At night, shine a bright light on a dark wall. Use your hands to make shadow puppets. In heaven nothing will block God's light.

❦ Spend an hour after dark trying to do things around your house without turning on a light. In heaven there will be no night. God's light will always shine.

❦ See how bright you can make a room. Let the sun stream in. Turn on every light. Shine flashlights, nightlights, and lamps. Light candles. In heaven God's light will shine brighter than all the brightest lights combined, and we will be filled with His radiance.

❦ When you are sitting in church, notice how the symbols in the stained glass windows appear more vivid as the sun shines more brightly. How do they appear when the sun is not so bright?

Our Response to God's Grace

Dear Christ, our Radiant Light,

We look forward with excitement to seeing You in heaven where Your light will fill us with Your glory. In Your name we pray. Amen.

Ponderings

☙ *The Light of God is glorious, majestic, radiant.* Psalm 76:4 reads, "You are resplendent with light, more majestic than mountains rich with game."

☙ *The light of God is a comfort to the afflicted.* Psalm 27:1 reads, "The Lord is my light and my salvation—whom shall I fear?"

↩ *God's light banishes darkness, replacing it with light.* Psalm 18:28 reads, "You, O Lord, keep my lamp burning; my God turns my darkness into light."

↩ *God's light is life.* Psalm 56:13 reads, "For You have delivered me from death and my feet from stumbling, that I may walk before God in the light of life."

↩ *God has given us His light here on earth, but in heaven we shall receive the fullness of God's light.* Revelation 22:5 reads, "There will be no more night. They will not need the light of a lamp or the light of the sun, for the Lord God will give them light. And they will reign forever and ever."

↩ Praise be to God for His glorious light!

Journal Jottings

Sunsets and Seasons

God's Grace to Us

Today's Reading: Genesis 1:14–19

And God said, "Let there be lights in the expanse of the sky to separate day from night, and let them serve as signs to mark seasons and days and years." Genesis 1:14

Faith Walk

Take an evening walk to a place with a good view for watching the sunset. Notice the various ways the colors in the sky change as the sun sets closer and closer to the horizon.

Faith Talk

✧ Sunsets are a part of the cycle of day and night, spring, summer, autumn, and winter, and the changing of the years. God created the sun, moon, and stars to be signs of seasons, days, and years.

✧ God created a world of order with seasons and cycles, patterns and rhythms. What rhythms do you see in the world around you?

✧ God's world of perfect order, of perfect harmony, was broken with chaos when sin entered the world.

✧ God is a God of love and grace, and so He set into motion a plan to not let sin completely destroy the world. We can still find sources of His goodness in the world. What good things have been in your life? The greatest good we find is the goodness of Jesus' death on the cross.

✧ At the end of the world, Jesus will return everything to perfect order.

Follow-up Activities

✤ On a sunny day, place a large object, such as a box, outside. Position it to face the setting sun. Compare the warmth of the side facing the sun to the warmth of Christ's love. Now compare the coolness of the side away from the sun to the lack of warmth we have apart from God.

✤ Choose a flowerbed, a tree, or a vegetable garden and keep a weekly record of how the sun shines on that spot at 6 P.M. Keep the record for at least three months, preferably a year. What rhythms do you see?

✤ At the library, research local weather conditions for the past two years. What patterns do you see?

✤ Take a photograph of a spot in your yard each hour from sunrise to sunset. What differences do you notice?

✤ Write an essay or poem comparing the seasons.

Our Response to God's Grace

Dear God our Creator,

You made day and night, seasons and years. For this we thank and praise You. Help us to remember that although You change the world each season, Your love for us will never change. In Jesus' name. Amen.

Ponderings

✐ Reflect on the following prayer:
Dear Creator of the Seasons, Days, and Years,
Thank You for the patterns of each day.
Thank You for the rising of the sun in the morning and its setting in the evening.
Thank You for the patterns of the seasons.
Thank You for the newness of spring, summer's warmth, the crispness of autumn, and winter's glistening snow.
Thank You for the patterns of life—the new life of a baby, the smiles of a child, the dreams of youth, and the wisdom of age.
Thank You, O Lord, for the patterns of life that give us comfort. Amen.

- Reflect on the rhythms of your life. In what ways has God positively touched you through them?

- Think of a time that the rhythm of your world was broken with pain and suffering. What role did God play in restoring rhythm during that time in your life?

- God created a perfect world of harmony and order. With the entry of sin into the world came discord, disharmony, and chaos. Sin caused the world to begin to collapse inward on itself. But God did not allow the world to completely collapse. He saved us from the eternal punishment of sin and, through His grace, it is still possible for us to enjoy beauty and pleasure within a certain semblance of order.

- God is love and with love comes tranquility. The opposite of love is hate and the bedfellow of hate is sin, which produces chaos. In the present world, love and hate, tranquility and chaos, God and sin, are in a constant tension with one another. But through Jesus Christ the war has been won! Jesus conquered sin on the cross and when Jesus returns, sin and chaos will be thrown into the abyss and tranquility and perfection shall reign for eternity!

Journal Jottings

Starry Night

God's Grace to Us

Today's Reading: Daniel 12:1–4

Those who are wise will shine like the brightness of the heavens, and those who lead many to righteousness, like the stars for ever and ever. Daniel 12:3

Faith Walk

Take a walk outside on a clear night in an area where there are few lights. Look for the brightest star.

Faith Talk

✧ Gaze at the stars for a while and talk about what you see.

✧ What do today's Bible verses say about the end of the world?

✧ What is wisdom? (Read Psalm 111:10.) What is meant by "Those who are wise will shine?"

✧ What does "lead many to righteousness" mean? What will happen to those who "lead many to righteousness?"

✧ How can you "shine like stars"? Who shines in you? It is only by Jesus' power that we can shine like stars.

✧ How can going to church and hearing God's Word keep you connected to this source of power?

Follow-up Activities

❈ Start a family collection of stars. Your collection might include stickers, pictures, books, postcards, and sequins. What else can you add to the collection? Be creative!

- ✤ Purchase a set of glow-in-the-dark star ceiling decorations. Put some on the ceilings of the children's rooms as a reminder that because of Jesus' death on the cross our faith shines both here on earth and into eternity.
- ✤ How many different ways you can draw pictures of stars?
- ✤ Make a "wisdom collage." Have each family member cut out and glue to a sheet of paper pictures that are reminders of wisdom. Give each person a turn to explain the pictures he or she chose.
- ✤ Create a star sticker book. Every time you see a Baptism in church or learn of someone becoming a Christian through Baptism, add a star.

Our Response to God's Grace

Dear God, Father of Eternity,

Thank You for sending Jesus to die for me and for giving me Your Spirit so I may someday enter Your kingdom. Help me to lead others to the righteousness that comes through faith in Jesus so they too may enter Your kingdom, and together we may radiate Your glory forever. In the radiance of Christ. Amen.

Ponderings

- ✐ *Light begets light.* Read Luke 8:16–18. God's light within us shines forth and draws others into the light of Christ's forgiveness, thereby creating more light. Light begets light.

- ✐ *Glory begets glory.* Read 2 Corinthians 3:7–18. The Law, given to Moses as the Ten Commandments, was glorious because it was righteousness. But because of the sinfulness of man and his inability to keep the righteousness of the Law, the glory of the Law quickly faded. Because we have been made righteous through Christ, the glory that is ours through faith in Christ does not fade. Rather, the Holy Spirit transforms us into the likeness of Christ and increases His glory. Glory begets glory.

- ✐ *Wisdom begets wisdom.* Read 1 Corinthians 1–2. The wisdom of the world, which denies the crucified Christ, is foolishness to God. The true wisdom is

"Christ the power of God." For those who believe, the Spirit has given this wisdom so we may know the mind of Christ. Wisdom begets wisdom.

✐ *Light begets light; glory begets glory; and wisdom begets wisdom.* The Holy Spirit working in us creates greater glory, honor, wisdom, and spiritual wealth not only in us, but also in those people whose spirits we touch so when we shine in heaven, God will be glorified.

✐ Pray that your works, done through faith in Jesus Christ and created by the Holy Spirit, may glorify God into eternity.

Journal Jottings

Heat Wave

God's Grace to Us

Today's Reading: Revelation 3:14–15

"I know your deeds, that you are neither cold nor hot." Revelation 3:15a

Faith Walk

Go on a long hike on a hot day. As a safety measure, take along some drinking water.

Faith Talk

✧ Talk about what it felt like to be hiking in the sun.

✧ When something is frozen, it is stiff. It does not move. But fire cannot be contained. It moves quickly, spreading rapidly. What does it mean to be spiritually hot or cold?

✧ How can the actions of a church or individual be hot, cold, or lukewarm?

✧ When Jesus died on the cross for us, He was showing us a blazing love. Now He desires that we love Him with a fiery love that cannot help but spread to others. How can you be "hot for Christ"?

Follow-up Activities

❋ Boil a pot of water, then set it aside for an hour. Have each person test it with a finger. What happened to the water? If you do not keep heating water, it cools. People are like water. If we do not fuel our faith with the fire of God's Word, we will become lukewarm Christians.

❋ Fill a pot half full with water. Measure the water depth, then boil it for half an hour. Measure the depth again. What was the difference? If you continue to boil the water, it will evaporate away. Likewise, if we burn the fire of our lives and do not add the Water of Life—Christ's Word—we will burn out.

🍁 Make a list of the ways you can stay connected to God's Word. Did you remember to include church? Make a list of the people who lead you to God's Word, helping to keep the fire of your faith burning. Did you remember to add your pastor, Sunday school teacher, and parents?

🍁 Write a list of ways to physically warm up when you are cold. Next write a list of ways to warm up when spiritually cold, such as reading God's Word or going to church. Keep your spiritual list posted as a reminder of the ways God works His fire in you.

🍁 Create a "news clip" describing a real or imaginary church that the Holy Spirit has changed from lukewarm to hot.

🍁 Write a prayer asking God's Spirit to be alive and active in your church and that your church be on fire for Christ. Give the prayer to church members and ask them to pray it daily.

Our Response to God's Grace

Dear Spirit of God,

You stand at our hearts and knock. Come into our hearts and build a blazing fire of Your love so the spirits of others might be warmed and our faith in Christ may spread like a fire until the whole world is filled with You! For Jesus' sake. Amen.

Ponderings

🍂 *Meditate on God's Spirit in you.* Has your spirit been blazing with God, lukewarm like a tepid bath, or one of the frozen chosen? Pray that God's Spirit strengthen your strengths, fill your needs, and overcome your weaknesses to make you mighty in Him. Pray that you will continuously seek the physical presence of His fiery love as you dine at His altar. Pray that God's Spirit blaze ever more strongly in you!

🍂 *Meditate on God's Spirit in your family.* Pray for each family member. What do they need spiritually? How are they strong? Thank God for the faith He has given each person in your family. Thank Him for their strengths and ask Him to overcome their weaknesses. Pray that God's Spirit blaze ever more strongly in your family!

✎ *Meditate on God's Spirit in your church.* If your church is on fire for the Lord, thank Him for His flame and ask Him for even more burning love. If your church struggles with apathy, pray fervently that God save her from spiritual death and ignite her faith on fire. Pray that God's Spirit blaze ever more strongly in your church!

✎ Reread the Scripture selection. What is the result of spiritual apathy?

✎ What rich reward—blessing—is promised to those who overcome? Memorize verse 21 and carry it in your heart to pull out when you get discouraged. Christ overcame sin and death on the cross. What an awesome reason to be on fire for the Lord!

Journal Jottings

Furnace of Fire

God's Grace to Us

Today's Reading: Daniel 3

[The king said,] "Look! I see four men walking around in the fire, unbound and unharmed, and the fourth looks like a son of the gods." Daniel 3:25

Faith Walk

Walk through a wooded area or park looking for materials, such as dry paper or twigs, and build a fire in a grill or fire ring. Toast marshmallows in the fire. Be sure to burn one.

Faith Talk

✦ Retell the story of The Three Men in the Fiery Furnace.

✦ Compare the fiery furnace to the campfire. How are they the same? Different?

✦ As you look at the burnt marshmallow, talk about what usually happens to someone in a fire. Why were Shadrach, Meshach, and Abednego unharmed in the fiery furnace even though it killed the soldiers who threw them in?

✦ God is with us when we are in the middle of the fires of painful times. Sometimes He rescues us from the fires right away; other times He watches and waits as He helps us endure the fires. Always, He loves us. And always, even when situations bring us pain, He knows and does what is best for us. Even when we do not understand why God does not remove us from a painful situation, we can trust Him to hold us in His arms and carry us through the pain. After all, God sent His Son to suffer the worst pain for us on the cross.

✦ What "fires" have you had in your life? How has God helped you through these fiery times?

Follow-up Activities

✤ Act out the story of The Three Men and the Fiery Furnace.

✤ Write the letters F-A-I-T-H on the fingers of one hand as a reminder of the faith God gave Shadrach, Meshach, and Abednego when they faced a fiery furnace and the faith He provides us in difficulties.

✤ Have each family member choose to be one character from the Bible story and take turns interviewing one another about your character's thoughts during the events of the story.

✤ Role-play situations in which you might be pressured to deny your faith, such as friends teasing you.

✤ Put a fireplace log on or near your home altar as a reminder of God's presence during life's fires.

Our Response to God's Grace

Dear Faithful Father,

Help us, when we are mistreated for our faith or are facing other "fires" in our lives, to cling to our faith and to Your loving hands which hold us. Through Jesus Christ, our Lord. Amen.

Ponderings

✐ "As soon as you hear the sound of the horn, flute, lyre, harp, pipes, and all kinds of music ..." (Daniel 3:5a). What sirens do we hear today calling us to worship false gods? Television? Movies? Our co-workers?

✐ "You must fall down and worship ..." (Daniel 3:5b). How does our society fall down to worship its false gods?

✐ "The image of gold that King Nebuchadnezzar has set up" (Daniel 3:5c). What are the false gods of our society? Of your family? Of your heart?

✐ "Whoever does not fall down and worship will immediately be thrown into a blazing furnace" (Daniel 3:6). What consequences do we face when we do not bow down to the gods of our society? While we may not face execution for bowing out of worship to false gods, the pressure to be "politically correct" or the desensitization with which we struggle can be a powerful force in luring many Christians down the path to idol worship.

🖋 "Praise be to the God of Shadrach, Meshach, and Abednego, who has sent His angel and rescued His servants!" (Daniel 3:28a). Praise be to Christ who died that we might be forgiven and who sent His Spirit to rescue us, His servants! May God's Holy Spirit abide in you so you may abide in Him!

Journal Jottings

September

september

Labor and Rest

God's Grace to Us

Today's Reading: Exodus 20:8–11

Six days you shall labor and do all your work, but the seventh day is a Sabbath to the Lord your God. Exodus 20:9–10a

Faith Walk

Walk around a business district in your community. As you look at the different businesses, talk about the types of jobs that are part of each business.

Faith Talk

✧ Discuss the word "labor." What is labor? How and why do people labor? Why do you think Labor Day started?

✧ How can Christians, including children, glorify God through their labors?

✧ What does "Sabbath" mean? What makes a Sabbath day different from other days? Why do you think God commands us to take a Sabbath?

✧ How can we use the Sabbath to glorify God?

✧ God gave us a command to take a Sabbath rest as a gift of His love. It is important that we be productive members of our family, church, and society. But God also recognizes the need for physical and spiritual rest. Taking a Sabbath day gives us that time. It also gives us a time to focus our attention on worshipping, praising, and glorifying our Lord.

Follow-up Activities

❧ Create a family worship service for Labor Day; include a Bible reading, songs, and prayer.

- Refuel with fun. Have a Labor Day picnic or go to a Labor Day parade.
- Write a list of ways people labor. Thank God for all the workers in the world that help to make our lives healthier, safer, richer, and more rounded.
- Write a list of the ways your family labors. Thank God for each person's contribution to your family.
- Labor in fun. Work on a favorite hobby or project.

Our Response to God's Grace

Dear God our Father, Maker of all Labor and Time,

You labored for six days, creating the world, and rested on the seventh, enjoying Your creation. Now You have commanded that we do likewise. Help us to enjoy our work and our rest. Help us to take time to come into Your house to worship. Help us to fill up on Your Word and to glorify You through our work and in our rest. In the peace of Jesus. Amen.

Ponderings

☞ *Remember.* God wants us to remember. He wants us to remember the Sabbath Day, the day set aside for Him, and He wants us to remember to keep it holy. He wants us to remember His work for us—His creation and His redeeming work through Jesus Christ. *Remember.*

☞ *Worship.* God wants us to worship. Remember the Sabbath day and keep it holy. He wants us to take a Sabbath to worship "the Lord your God." On the Sabbath, we are to take our minds off our labors and focus them on our Lord. *Worship.*

☞ *Pattern.* God wants us to pattern our days after Him. "For in six days the Lord made the heavens and the earth, the sea, and all that is in them, but He rested on the seventh day. Therefore the Lord blessed the Sabbath day and made it holy" (Exodus 20:11). God's ways are an example for us. We are to pattern our lives after Him. He has ordained it and He has blessed it. *Pattern.*

☞ *Labor.* God wants us to labor. "Six days you shall labor and do all your work" (Deuteronomy 5:13). "For in six days the Lord made the heavens and the earth, the sea, and all that is in them ... ". We are to work, produce, and create. God has blessed us to be productive and expects us to use this blessing. *Labor.*

🖋 *Rest.* God wants us to rest. "On [the seventh day] you shall not do any work ..." (Deuteronomy 5:14b) "... but He rested on the seventh day." On the Sabbath, God wants us to rest so we may replenish our bodies and our spirits. On the Sabbath, we can center our lives on our God, our Maker, Creator, and Redeemer, and receive the true rest that comes not through works of righteousness but through faith in the redeeming work of a righteous and forgiving God. "For anyone who enters God's rest also rests from his own work, just as God did from His" (Hebrews 4:10). *Rest.*

Journal Jottings

Labor of Love

God's Grace to Us

Today's Reading: Ephesians 3:14–4:16

From Him the whole body, joined and held together by every supporting ligament, grows and builds itself up in love, as each part does its work. Ephesians 4:16

Faith Walk

Walk through your neighborhood looking for "labors of love"—homegrown projects lovingly done.

Faith Talk

✧ What is a "labor of love?"

✧ What was the greatest labor of love Christ did for us? Hint: Read John 19:17.

✧ How are our lives to be labors of love for Christ? For one another? Why?

✧ What happens through our labors of love? Reread and ponder today's Bible verse.

✧ Examine your lives. How can your lives better reflect labors of love for the Lord and for one another?

Follow-up Activities

❦ Have each family member carry around a heavy object, such as a brick, for several hours. At the end of the designated time discuss the experience. How did it feel? Is labor always easy?

❦ Have each person in your family try to lift a vehicle. Can it be done alone? Trying to live in perfect righteousness alone, without Jesus' forgiveness and the Holy Spirit working in our hearts, is impossible. We are weak because of our sin.

❦ Pass out helium-filled balloons. The Holy Spirit can be compared to the helium in the balloons. Christ took away the weight of our sins, and the Holy Spirit makes us weightless and lifts us up to do good deeds in Jesus' name.

❦ Use blocks to build something. Each block alone cannot make a grand construction, but together they can build a cathedral, a castle, or a mansion. Our labors of love alone may not seem to amount to much, but together they build up, in love, the body of Christ.

❦ Make a "Labor of Love Quilt." On colored index cards, write "Labors of Love" you can do for your family and glue the cards onto a poster board.

Our Response to God's Grace

Dear Christ, the Head of the Church,

May we, the body, labor in love for You, supporting one another and building up Your kingdom, just as You offered us the greatest labor of love, Your death. In Your name we pray. Amen.

Ponderings

☙ "How wide and long and high and deep is the love of Christ" (Ephesians 3:18b). Christ's love for us has no limits and knows no boundaries. It is deeper than our lowest lows, higher than our highest highs, and as wide as arms stretched out on a cross. Christ's love surpasses knowledge, yet is known to us through faith as it fills us to the measure of all fullness, lifting us up, and carrying us to the throne of God.

❧ "Now to Him who is able to do immeasurably more than all we ask or imagine, according to His power that is at work within us" (Ephesians 3:20). Christ's power at work within us has no limits, no boundaries. There is no task, no job, no challenge too hard for us to accomplish when we are connected to the power of Christ. For it is not us, but Christ within us, who is laboring to accomplish His goals.

❧ "To Him be glory in the church and in Christ Jesus throughout all generations, forever and ever! Amen" (Ephesians 3:21). With the love and power of Christ working within us we, together with all the church, lift up and glorify our Lord.

❧ "There is one body and one Spirit—just as you were called to one hope when you were called—one Lord, one faith, one Baptism, one God and Father of all, who is over all and through all and in all" (Ephesians 4:4). The church is one, a unified body of believers with the Father over, in, and through all. Our Father who created the world "in the beginning," has made a new creation—the body of Christ.

❧ "From Him the whole body, joined and held together by every supporting ligament, grows and builds itself up in love, as each part does its work" (Ephesians 4:16). The Christian church, under the headship and in the power and love of Christ, joins together as a body of believers building itself up in love through service to the glory of the Lord. May you live and work in that glory!

Journal Jottings

Festivals and Fairs

God's Grace to Us

Today's Reading: Song of Songs 2:4, 10–13

He has taken me to the banquet hall, and His banner over me is love. Song of Songs 2:4

Faith Walk

Take a walk through a Labor Day festival or end-of-summer fair. Enjoy some of the activities.

Faith Talk

✧ Describe some of the sights, sounds, and smells of the festival.

✧ What activities or events did you enjoy the most?

✧ The Bible passage reminds us that our relationship with God is a banquet, a feast, a festival of love.

✧ God gathers His children under His banner of love. This banner was proclaimed in Jesus' death.

✧ We can celebrate God's love for us with joy and delight.

Follow-up Activities

❧ Invite some friends over for a banquet of favorite foods. If you do not have time to prepare a full feast, have a brunch, an appetizer party, or a potluck. Share today's Scripture verse with your guests.

❧ Make a family banner proclaiming God's love for you.

❧ Sing a favorite song about God's love, such as "His Banner over Me Is Love" (*All God's People Sing!*, Concordia Publishing House, © 1992) or "You Can't Keep Jesus' Love in a Box" (*Little Ones Sing Praise*, Concordia Publishing House, © 1989).

❧ Heaven is described as a wedding banquet in Revelation 19:6–10. The bridegroom is Jesus, the bride is the church—the community of believers. Write and illustrate a poem showing how you imagine the heavenly wedding banquet.

❧ Put on some lively instrumental music and have a dance to celebrate God's love for us.

Our Response to God's Grace

Dear Loving Father,

We praise and thank You for the banner of love under which You gather us. We look forward to the wedding feast in heaven and being with Jesus, the Bridegroom. Until then may we walk in Your love, as we seek to love You in return. In His name, which is Love. Amen.

Ponderings

✒ Meditate on how you feast on God's love.

✒ How has God's banner over you been love?

✒ Love is not only a noun, it is a verb, an action. In what ways has God acted in your life to show you His love?

✒ Read the entire Old Testament book of Song of Songs. As you do, ask yourself, "What is God saying in this book about the relationship between a husband and wife?"

✒ Read Song of Songs a second time. This time ask yourself, "How can the Song of Songs be compared to the relationship between God and His bride, the church? Between God and me?"

Journal Jottings

Outdoor Education

God's Grace to Us

Today's Reading: Proverbs 1:1–9

Let the wise listen and add to their learning. Proverbs 1:5

Faith Walk

Turn on your senses, rev up your mind, awaken your awareness, and take a walk with the goal of seeing, hearing, noticing, questioning, and learning everything you can. Pay attention to the smallest details of a crack in the sidewalk or the shape of a tree branch. The goal of your walk is to study and learn about everything around you.

Faith Talk

✧ What did you learn?

✧ What did you learn about learning?

✧ God has given us a world full of mysteries and glimpses into His nature. By studying and learning, we can grow closer to God.

✧ Read verse seven of the Scripture reading. What is the key to knowledge?

✧ What is wisdom? How do we receive wisdom? The greatest wisdom is the wisdom that comes through a relationship with Jesus. Why?

Follow-up Activities

❧ Write a learning goal. Choose a subject that you want to learn more about and make a plan to study it. For example, if you want to learn more about space, you might read about it, watch television programs on space, and go to a museum with space exhibits. Try to pick a subject you know little about.

❧ The book of Proverbs describes wisdom as a woman. Find items in your home, such as jewels, that remind you of wisdom and share them with one another. Explain why you chose those objects.

❧ Start a family "wisdom journal." In it keep Bible verses, quotes, proverbs, stories, and insights about wisdom.

❧ Write a thank-you note to someone who has helped you to become wiser.

❧ Grow a crystal garden (see Appendix B for recipe). The Bible describes wisdom as jewels. When God's Word is poured into our hearts, His Spirit within us grows a garden filled with the crystals of wisdom, knowledge, and understanding of God's truths.

Our Response to God's Grace

Dear Holy Spirit, Giver of all Good Wisdom and Knowledge,

Please fill our hearts and minds with Your Word and help us to grow in wisdom, knowledge, and understanding of You and Your ways. Through Christ Jesus, our Lord. Amen.

Ponderings

✐ Write a definition of wisdom.

✐ Study the following Bible passages to expand and enrich your understanding of wisdom:

1 Kings 4:29–34
Isaiah 11:1–5
1 Corinthians 1:18–31
Romans 11:33–36
1 Corinthians 12:8

✐ Study the book of Proverbs and keep a journal of your insights.

✐ Wisdom is the ability to sense God in everything, to see with spiritual eyes, to hear the voice of the Lord, to be touched by the Spirit, and to taste the richness of God's most intimate love. As you see, hear, taste, touch, and experience the mundane and the profound, the painful and the joyful, the moments and the hours, keep your spirit open for God's wisdom crying out to you.

✍ Spend time in meditation and prayer seeking the wisdom of Solomon.

Journal Jottings

Crude Cross

God's Grace to Us

Today's Reading: Philippians 2:5–18

And being found in appearance as a man, He humbled Himself and became obedient to death—even death on a cross! Philippians 2:8

Faith Walk

On Holy Cross Day, September 14, walk through a park or down a tree-lined street to collect twigs that look like a cross or can be shaped to make a cross.

Faith Talk

✧ Holy Cross Day is a day to think about the cross of Christ and what it means for us.

✧ Jesus, who is God, humbled Himself. He became our servant and died the crudest and cruelest of deaths—death on a cross.

✧ Christ's humiliation—His death on a cross—also became His exaltation—His glory! God lifted Him up and every knee shall bow to Him, worship Him, and call Him Lord (Philippians 2:10)!

✧ Jesus' attitude is to be our attitude. Through the power of Jesus' death on the cross, He helps us become humble servants.

✧ We have received salvation through Jesus' death. Now, with God working in us, we are to grow in our faith, our salvation, so we might shine like stars and glorify Jesus. This is the meaning and power of the cross—not crudeness but glory!

Follow-up Activities

❧ Place your twig crosses on your home altar.

❧ Praise and glorify Jesus through a favorite hymn such as "Beautiful Savior" or "Shout to the Lord."

❧ Cut a large cross from poster board. Write some of your sins on slips of paper and tape them to the cross as a reminder that when Jesus was nailed to the cross, our sinfulness was nailed to the cross with Him.

❧ Practice humiliation by washing one another's feet at the end of a busy day. (See the story of Christ washing the feet of His disciples in John 13:1–17.) What did it feel like to have someone wash your feet? What did it feel like to wash someone else's feet? What do you think Jesus meant when He said, "I have set an example that you should do as I have done for you" (John 13:15)?

❧ Make a list of ways you can live as servants in the world and glorify Jesus. Role-play several ideas.

Our Response to God's Grace

Dear Christ, King of kings and Lord of lords,

You are King of all, Lord of all and God of all, yet You lowered Yourself to the lowest of deaths, the death of a criminal on the cross. Praise be that through Your death You have been lifted up and we have been freed from sin. O Lord, help us to continue to glorify You through our words and actions. In Your glorified name we pray. Amen.

Ponderings

❧ *Cross.* When you hear the word "cross," what story comes to mind? Read aloud Mark 15:20–40. What does this story teach us about God's grace to us? How does it give new meaning to the gift of forgiveness that is ours as we receive His body and blood in Holy Communion? Write down your insights.

❧ *Cross.* When you hear the word "cross," what image comes to mind? Read John 19:30 and Matthew 27:54. How do these images of Christ on the cross contrast? How do they illustrate this week's Scripture? Meditate on an image of Christ on the cross.

↬ *Cross.* When you hear the word "cross," what teachings come to mind? Study 1 Corinthians 1:18–31. What does it teach you about the cross of Christ?

↬ *Cross.* When you hear the word "cross," what feelings come to mind? Read Hebrews 12:2 and Colossians 1:19–20. How do Jesus and the Father view the cross? What does this say to you?

↬ *Cross.* When you hear the word "cross," what prayers come to mind? Read Matthew 17 for a look at the prayers Jesus prayed as He was preparing to be crucified. Spend time praying that these words and that the meaning and power of the cross may be opened to you.

Journal Jottings

Fruits of the Spirit

God's Grace to Us

Today's Reading: Galatians 5:22–26

But the fruit of the Spirit is love, joy, peace, patience, kindness, goodness, faithfulness, gentleness and self-control. Galatians 5:22–23a

Faith Walk

In September people are still harvesting the fruits of their gardens, bushes, and trees. Walk through your neighborhood looking for all the different fruits you can spot.

Faith Talk

✧ Good trees, bushes, and vines produce good fruits. Bad trees, bushes, and vines produce bad fruits. Describe the difference between a good fruit and a bad fruit.

✧ The fruits of faith are love, joy, peace, patience, kindness, goodness, faithfulness, gentleness, and self-control. Give some examples of how people use these fruits.

✧ When Jesus died, our sinful nature died with Him. We are now free from sin in God's eyes—we are free to do the good works of God's Spirit living in us. How has God helped you show good fruit in your life? What are some good fruits in your life?

Follow-up Activities

❦ Gift wrap a piece of fruit. Have one family member open it. Explain that the fruit of the Spirit is a gift. It is not something we do but a blessing from God's Spirit living in our hearts. It is the gift of righteousness. We have been made right with God through Jesus and so we freely, out of love, give back to Him our good deeds.

* Eat an ice cream sundae with fruit. How does the fruit of the Spirit sweeten our hearts and lives?

* Draw a Bible on a piece of poster board. Cut construction paper into the following shapes: apple, banana, grapes, orange, pear, peach, strawberry, watermelon, and pineapple (see Appendix B). Write a different fruit of the Spirit on each shape and glue the fruits around the Bible. We are rooted in the Spirit through God's Word and Christ Himself, who is the Word. As a result, we produce good fruit.

* Is there a fruit of the Spirit you struggle with the most as you try to show it in your daily life? Pray for God's Spirit to produce that fruit in your heart and life for the glory of Jesus.

* Make a fruit salad. As you eat it discuss the fruit of the Spirit.

Our Response to God's Grace

Dear Christ Jesus,

Thank You for the gift of Your Spirit, which produces in us good fruit. May Your Holy Spirit work in us to show love, joy, peace, patience, kindness, goodness, faithfulness, gentleness, and self-control in our lives. In Your name. Amen.

Ponderings

* Do a frank examination of your spiritual center. Write a description of your inner spiritual life.

* Read Psalm 51:1–5 and Romans 3:9–20. Use these passages to write a description of the human spirit.

- Read Ephesians 2:1–10. Our spirit, apart from Christ, is like the rotting flesh of a dead man. But thanks be to Christ that while we were still sinners His death purified us and made us alive!

- Through Christ and His Spirit dwelling in us, we are a new creation. To understand what it means to be a new creation, read 2 Corinthians 5:17–21, Ezekiel 36:25–27, and Ephesians 4:23–25.

- Through Baptism into Christ and His death we are a new creation. Our corrupt sinful self is dead and in its place is a holy and righteous self, producing good deeds and living freely in God's will. This is the fruit of the Spirit. The virtues that result are love, joy, peace, patience kindness, goodness, faithfulness, gentleness, and self-control. Spend time in prayer asking God's Spirit to continue the good work begun in you so you may become more like Him and reflect Him in your life and actions. Examine your behaviors and ask also that He strengthen those areas in which you are weak. To Him be the glory and power!

- Examine how often you come into God's presence through worship, drinking in His Word, and the gifts of His grace. Reenergize and reconnect with frequent trips to His altar so you might be empowered to live out these fruits of your faith in Christ.

Journal Jottings

October

Fields Are Ripe

God's Grace to Us

Today's Reading: Matthew 9:35–38

Then [Jesus] said to His disciples, "The harvest is plentiful but the workers are few. Ask the Lord of the harvest, therefore, to send out workers into His harvest field." Matthew 9:37–38

Faith Walk

Walk through a field, an orchard, a vegetable garden, or a neighborhood with gardens. Note how the fruits or vegetables are ripe and ready to be picked.

Faith Talk

✧ What happens at harvest time?

✧ What does it mean to "harvest" the souls of people?

✧ The harvest is plentiful. There are many people who need to hear the Good News of salvation in Christ and be brought to God so He might work faith in their hearts.

✧ Who are some of the workers in God's kingdom? Who spreads the Good News of salvation to others? Pastors? Missionaries? Teachers? Parents? You?

✧ The workers are few. The kingdom of God needs us and others to reach out to the unsaved with the Word of God and bring them into the kingdom.

✧ "Ask the Lord of the harvest therefore, to send out workers into the harvest field." We are to pray for more missionaries—people who spread God's Word in their families, neighborhoods, cities, and abroad.

✧ How could God work through your family to lift up your pastor and others you know who spread the Good News?

Follow-up Activities

✤ Enjoy a family-day-out, picking fruit at an orchard.

✤ Visit a farmer's market or specialty grocery store and look for unfamiliar produce. Bring home a new fruit or vegetable to try.

✤ Take a picture of a ripe field or orchard. Post the picture as a reminder that the fields are ripe.

✤ Write a thank-you note to your pastor for all He does in God's kingdom. Pray for him and pray that there will be more and more pastors to preach God's Word near and far.

✤ Pray for each continent, asking for missionaries to be sent there and for the fields to be harvested.

✤ Ask that God will help your family be missionaries to your neighborhood. Brainstorm ways to get to know your neighbors and share your faith with them.

Our Response to God's Grace

Dear Heavenly Father, Lord of the Harvest,

The fields are ripe and the laborers are few. Please, O Lord, send more workers into the field. Stir hearts to become pastors and missionaries, open mouths to speak Your words, and give power to the faithful, including us, to bring more people to You. For Jesus' sake. Amen.

Ponderings

✑ *There is work to be done.* There are children to be nurtured, babies to be sung to, tables to be set, floors to be mopped, teenagers to be heard, sick to be visited, elderly people to be transported, hearts and souls to be touched. *There is work to be done.*

✑ *More workers are needed.* The harvest is ready. The crops are plentiful. The produce will rot on the vines if it is not picked. But the workers are few and their time is short. Fear, consumerism, apathy, abundant recreation, and responsibilities—real and imagined—all eat away at the time, energy, and people resources needed to harvest the fields. *More workers are needed.*

- *Your hands are needed.* Your hands are needed to heal the hurting, serve the hungry, clean the churches, wipe the noses and wash the bottoms of infants, and to build education wings or sew quilts. Every labor of love is valuable and essential. *Your hands are needed.*

- *Your voice is needed.* Your voice is needed to comfort the afflicted. Your voice is needed to share God's Word and sing His praise, to pray for new workers and to encourage tired workers. *Your voice is needed.*

- *The Spirit is needed.* The Spirit is needed to call you, equip you, and empower you for His work. The Spirit is needed to lift you up when you are down and to work through you when you feel inadequate. The Spirit is needed to enter the hearts of those who do not know God and to bring them into the kingdom. *The Spirit is needed.*

- *Yes, we are needed. No, we are not left alone to do God's work.* It is the work of God's Spirit to harvest the fields. We are His tools. Read Joel 2:28–32. God's Spirit is needed and God's Spirit is promised.

Journal Jottings

Crown of Life

God's Grace to Us

Today's Reading: 1 Peter 5:4, 9–10

And when the Chief Shepherd appears, you will receive the crown of glory that will never fade away. 1 Peter 5:4

Faith Walk

Take a walk to examine the fall leaves. Look for leaves that are still green, those that are bright red, orange or yellow, and some that are brown.

Faith Talk

✧ Discuss what happens to leaves in the fall. Most leaves begin as a deep green color. Then they burst into brilliant shades of yellow, red, and orange, but quickly their colors fade into the drab brown of a dead leaf.

✧ People without faith are like leaves. They may lead glamorous lives that look good on the outside but when they die, their glory fades away.

✧ God has given all who believe in Christ a promise. We will be given an eternal crown of life that will not fade.

✧ Read 1 Peter 1:3–9 for a picture of our never-fading glory in Jesus.

Follow-up Activities

❧ Place one green leaf, one brilliant red, yellow, or orange leaf, and one dead brown leaf on your home altar.

❧ Make a leaf collection. To preserve the leaves, iron them between sheets of waxed paper. Cover the waxed paper with newspaper while you iron to keep from melting wax onto your iron.

- Do leaf rubbings. Place leaves, vein-side-up, under a piece of paper. Rub over the leaves with the sides of crayons. Be sure to rub over the entire leaf for the full effect.

- Make crowns from paper and green leaves. How long does it take for their glory to fade?

- As a reminder that all glory comes from God, sing a praise song such as "The King of Glory" (*All God's People Sing!*, Concordia Publishing House, 1992).

Our Response to God's Grace

Dear Christ, King of Glory,

When we get discouraged, help us to remember the glory that awaits us in heaven through the glory and power of Your death on the cross. To You be the glory! For Your sake. Amen.

Ponderings

- *Glory to the Father!* By His word He created the heavens and the earth. He gives salvation to the just and brings judgment to the wicked. We praise His name! Read Revelation 4:9–11 and 19:1–4. What do these words reveal about the glory of the Father?

- *Glory to the Lamb!* He loves us, has freed us by His blood, and will return for us. Hallelujah! Praise be to the Savior! Read Revelation 1:5b-8, 5:6–14, and 19:6–9. What do these words reveal about the glory of the Lamb?

- *Glory to the Spirit!* God's Perfect Spirit gives us the words of eternal life. Praise and glory to the Spirit of Life! Read Revelation 2:7 and 4:1–6. What do these words reveal about the glory of the Spirit?

- All glory be to God the Father, Son, and Holy Spirit, who will reign in the New Jerusalem—heaven! Read about the New Jerusalem in Revelation 22. What do these words reveal about the glory of God's kingdom?

- Through the blood of Christ, we will receive a crown of glory and live with Him in heaven for all eternity! This promise is made through Baptism as the names of God's own are written in the Book of Life. Read and learn about our role in the glory of the kingdom of God in Revelation 7:9–17, 14:1–5, and 22:1–6. The glory of God shall never fade! Alleluia! Amen.

Journal Jottings

Wings like Eagles

God's Grace to Us

Today's Reading: Isaiah 40:28–31

But those who hope in the LORD will renew their strength. They will soar on wings like eagles; they will run and not grow weary, they will walk and not be faint. Isaiah 40:31

Faith Walk

Walk to a spot where flocks of migrating or congregating birds can be easily observed.

Faith Talk

✧ Close your eyes and imagine soaring like the birds. Describe what you see, feel, and think.

✧ Most birds fly easily, without much effort. Once they learn as babies it comes natural to them.

✧ What does Isaiah mean when he promises that those who hope in the Lord will soar like eagles?

✧ We are often weighed down by problems—a bad grade on a test, problems with friends, a fight with a family member, illness, or accidents. What problems do you struggle with in your life?

✧ Hold in your hearts the promise that you can hope in the Lord because He will lift you up on wings of an eagle! What will happen to your problems as you hope in the Lord?

Follow-up Activities

❧ Have a high jump contest. Think how much higher an eagle can fly!

❧ Cut a picture of an eagle from a magazine or book, or download a picture from the Internet. Glue the picture on a piece of construction paper and display it as a reminder of this verse.

❧ Run until you grow weary. Close your eyes and think about what it means to not grow weary.

❧ Write all your worries on a piece of paper, and pray that God will give you the strength to not grow weary in your troubles. Throw the paper away.

❧ Visit an aviary, bird sanctuary, or other spot where an abundance of birds take refuge. Observe the birds flying and meditate on this passage from God's Word.

Our Response to God's Grace

Dear Father, God of Power, Strength, and Comfort,

When we are struggling with burdens, we can wait and hope in You, for You will lift us up on wings like eagles. You have promised to give us strength. Help us to take comfort, and be strengthened in our faith in Your Son as we remember Your promise. Through Jesus we pray. Amen.

Ponderings

☙ *He will not grow tired and weary.* We may grow tired and weary from the struggles and hardships of life, but not God. Jesus says, "Come to Me, all you who are weary and burdened, and I will give you rest ... for My yoke is easy and My burden is light" (Matthew 11:28 and 30). *I am weak but He is strong.*

☙ *His understanding no one can fathom.* God's understanding runs deeper than my weariness, pain, and sorrow. God felt the pain I feel, walked the road I walk, and took the burdens I carry when He took the form of man and carried my burdens to the cross. He heals my hurt and has compassion on my grief. *I am weak but He is strong.*

🖎 *He gives strength to the weary.* I do not have to rest on my strength alone. On God I rest. God the Creator is stronger than the creation. God's strength is my strength. *I am weak but He is strong.*

🖎 *Those who hope in the Lord will renew their strength.* I have hope. Even when my strength is failing and God's strength seems far off, I have hope. He will renew—make new—my strength. In God's promise I rest. *I am weak but He is strong.*

🖎 *They will soar on wings like eagles.* God will lift me above my problems, give me wings to fly, and I will soar, effortlessly, above the horizon. I will run and not grow weary. I will walk and not be faint. God's strength and power will be my freedom and flight! *I am weak but He is strong!*

Journal Jottings

Pumpkin Patch

God's Grace to Us

Today's Reading: Colossians 1:3–14

All over the world this Gospel is bearing fruit and growing, just as it has been doing among you since the day you heard it and understood God's grace in all its truth. Colossians 1:6

Faith Walk

Explore a pumpkin patch. Check out the soil, the vines, and the leaves. Look for pumpkins of different sizes. See how many stages of growth you can find.

Faith Talk

✧ From one pumpkin seed grows a vine that produces a number of pumpkins.

✧ The pumpkin vine spreads through the pumpkin patch.

✧ The seed of God's Word, the Gospel, bears the fruit of believers.

✧ The Christian church has spread through the world, producing believers on every continent.

✧ We can help to grow the fruit of believers by sharing the Gospel with everyone we meet.

Follow-up Activities

✤ Carve a cross in a pumpkin and set it on your front steps or in a window as a symbol to those who pass by.

✤ Place a candle inside the pumpkin and recall that Christ calls us to be a light of His Gospel.

✤ Clean and dry pumpkin seeds. After they have dried, brush them with oil, sprinkle them with salt, and toast them in the oven at 325° for 10 minutes. Remember that the seed of faith begins with God's Word.

✤ Have a pumpkin party. Serve toasted pumpkin seeds, pumpkin pie, and hot apple cider. Make a poster board pumpkin and play "Pin the Nose on the Jack-o-Lantern." Use paints to decorate pumpkins with Christian symbols. Make pictures by gluing a design of pumpkin seeds onto heavy paper and coloring the design with markers.

✤ To explore other Christian teachings that can be learned through the example of a pumpkin, read *The Pumpkin Patch Parable* by Liz Curtis Higgs (Thomas Nelson Inc., 1995).

Our Response to God's Grace

Dear Jesus, our True Vine,

You are the Vine; we are the branches. It is the Gospel of Your love for us that bears fruit. Help us, like the pumpkin plant, to spread Your Gospel through the world. In Your name. Amen.

Ponderings

☞ The pumpkin vine wanders. The dandelion seeds blow. The bee busily flits from flower to flower, spreading pollen. The apple tree spreads its branches until it sags under the weight of apples. The raspberry bush sends shoots to other parts of the yard. Growth. Without the wind to blow the seeds, the sun to shine, the rain to fall, and the nourishing nutrients of the soil, growth would not occur and soon the plants would die. What can we learn from plants about spiritual growth and the spread of the Gospel?

☞ Jesus says, "I am the true vine." Read His words about growth and the spread of the Gospel in John 15:1–17. How can Christ use us? What is our role in the growth of the church?

☞ Reread Paul's words in Colossians 1:6: "This Gospel is bearing fruit and growing." Spend time praying and meditating on this passage. What does Paul mean by the Gospel bearing fruit?

↜ What role has God called you to play in the spreading of His Word? Pray and meditate on this question. Spend time listening for God's answer. As you earnestly seek the answer to this question, consider your gifts and talents, your time and energy, your skills, resources, and training, and the ministry areas that touch your spirit.

↜ Whether or not you feel a strong calling to an area of ministry, God desires that you bear fruit. Pray for God's wisdom, guidance, and empowerment as you seek to do His will and spread His Gospel.

Journal Jottings

Ghosts and Goblins

God's Grace to Us

Today's Reading: 1 John 4:1–6

You, dear children, are from God and have overcome them, because the One who is in you is greater than the one who is in the world. 1 John 4:4

Faith Walk

Walk through your neighborhood looking for Halloween decorations that show scary things such as witches, ghosts, and goblins.

Faith Talk

✧ Many people consider "Halloween spooks" to be innocent fun. But some stretch the limits because Satan's presence in the world is not innocent fun. He and his angels are real.

✧ It is important that we know the difference between spirits from God and messengers of Satan. Anyone or anything that declares that Jesus is God in the flesh is from God. Anything or anyone who does not proclaim Jesus is not from God.

✧ We need to be aware of the false spirits and stand against them. But we do not need to be afraid of them. Jesus conquered the false spirits by His death on the cross! God is more powerful than all other spirits and He is in us, giving us His strength.

✧ The world listens to false spirits. We listen to the voice of God. We hear God's voice through His Words in the Bible.

✧ This Halloween, instead of focusing on witches, ghosts, and goblins, focus on the Spirit of God.

Follow-up Activities

♣ Memorize the Bible verse and call upon it when you feel worried. To help memorize the verse, break it into sections and say it as an echo prayer.

♣ Read Ephesians 6:10–18. Decorate your home, not with witches, ghosts, and goblins, but with the armor of God (see pages 296–300 in Appendix B for patterns).

♣ Read some newspaper stories and discuss the things that are done or said. Are these words and actions from God or from false teachers?

♣ Gather several reference books. What is the purpose of these books? They inform people about different subjects. God's Word, the Bible, informs people about God's will. God's Word is more than just a reference book—it has power, the power of God to fight Satan and his angels. When we strengthen ourselves with God's Word, Satan cannot overpower us.

♣ Sing "A Mighty Fortress Is Our God."

Our Response to God's Grace

Dear Spirit of Truth,

Help us to know the difference between Your truths and the false ideas or teachings of others. Help us to fight Satan with Your Word. And comfort us with Your strength. In the power of Jesus. Amen.

Ponderings

✐ John warns his readers to test every spirit. How can you help your children learn to discern between godly values and teachings and ungodly values and teachings?

✐ The first step in discernment is knowledge. John gives his readers knowledge by teaching them that the litmus test for godly versus ungodly spirits is whether they acknowledge that Jesus Christ came into the world as God and man. How can you arm your children with the knowledge they need to be discerning and wise?

❧ John comforts his readers with the knowledge that God is in them and God is stronger than any one in the world. Read Luke 10:17. Even the name of Jesus can make Satan flee! How can you help your children take comfort in God's power when they face evil?

❧ John addresses his readers as "dear children" nine times in five chapters. Five times he calls us "children of God." And he uses the term "born of God" nine times. He also tells us that "God lives in us," "we are from God," and "God's seed remains in us." We have been born of God and are God's own through Baptism. John emphasizes, repeatedly, the presence of God in our lives. We are not left alone to fight the evil spirits of the world. God in us fights the battles for us!

❧ Pray for knowledge and wisdom, comfort and strength for your children.

Journal Jottings

Reverse Halloween Walk

God's Grace to Us

Today's Reading: Isaiah 52:7–10

How beautiful on the mountains are the feet of those who bring good news, who proclaim peace, who bring good tidings, who proclaim salvation, who say to Zion, "Your God reigns!" Isaiah 52:7

Faith Walk

Go on a "Reverse Halloween Walk." On Halloween dress in costumes and walk door-to-door handing out tracts, booklets, pencils, or other items that proclaim the Good News of salvation through Jesus. If it is a family custom to trick-or-treat, you might choose to give these out as you receive candy and say "Trade-a-treat!"

Faith Talk

✧ In the days of Isaiah, messengers ran to deliver the news from a battle. When the news was good—that they had won the battle, were delivered from their enemies, and peace would return—the messengers were greeted with joy.

✧ As you walk door-to-door, you are like a messenger that is delivering news from a battle. Your news is Good News—that Christ has won the battle over sin, death, and the devil. Your feet are delivering the Good News that we have peace and salvation through Jesus!

✧ How does Jesus bring us peace and salvation?

Follow-up Activities

❧ Have a good news week. Keep a list of all the good news your family has this week. At the end of the week have a special prayer praising God for the good news He has placed in your lives, especially the Good News of Christ.

✤ Write an article for your church newsletter explaining this week's Bible passage and Good News. Tell about your reverse Halloween walk and offer ideas for how people in your church might continue to spread the Good News in new and fun ways.

✤ Make a sign declaring the Good News of Jesus and post it in your front yard for trick-or-treaters to see.

✤ Create your own Good News tracts to give out on Halloween.

✤ Hand out your Good News items not only to the homes you visit but also to those who visit your home.

Our Response to God's Grace

Dear Father, God of all Salvation,

Please help us to spread the message that Jesus has won the battle against Satan and we are free! Help us to be Good News messengers, bringing the message of God's peace and salvation to all who hear us. For the sake of Christ. Amen.

Ponderings

✍· How beautiful are the feet of those who bring good news. You are parched; dried like a baked brick. You have no shelter. The sun blazes on you at temperatures as high as 120 degrees. Unexpectedly someone appears with a bucket of ice water and promises that the bucket will never run dry. How beautiful are the feet of those who bring good news!

✍· Christ has appeared to us with a bucket of ice water to quench our thirsting souls. His water is the water of life given to us by His death on the cross. Read John 4:7–14. Meditate on your soul's thirst and how the Living Water quenches that thirst.

✍· Reread Isaiah 52:7–10, paying attention to the blessings that arrive with the Good News. Rewrite this passage, applying it to your own life in the light of the Gospel of Jesus.

✍· We have been given the Good News of salvation and can rejoice in it. But not everyone has received the message that God reigns victorious over sin, death, and the power of the devil and that His victory is the victory of all who trust in Jesus as their Savior. Therefore it is imperative that we be messengers bringing the Good News to all corners of the earth.

Jesus brought the Good News to the woman at the well by building a relationship with her. While signs, tracts, and door-to-door evangelism may bring God's Word to some people, it is through our relationships that we can best be the bearers of Good News. To whom can you be a messenger?

Journal Jottings

November

november

Changing Days——Changeless Jesus

God's Grace to Us

Today's Reading: Hebrews 13:8, 20–21

Jesus Christ is the same yesterday and today and forever. Hebrews 13:8

Faith Walk

As winter draws near, many changes take place in nature. Walk through a park, nature preserve, or farm, and look for the changes in nature that hint at the coming of winter.

Faith Talk

✧ What changes did you find?

✧ What changes have you made in your lives?

✧ How do you feel about change?

✧ Jesus never changes. He is changeless. The same Jesus that walked the earth and laughed, cried, healed, loved, and died on the cross so we might live forever, continues to walk among us.

✧ What does a changeless Jesus mean to you?

Follow-up Activities

❧ Look at baby pictures of each family member and talk about the ways you have changed.

❧ Try to predict the future. Imagine yourselves 20 years from now. What do you imagine you will look like, act like, and be doing in 20 years? Write out your predictions and seal them in a time capsule or box to be opened in 20 years.

❧ Create a mini art gallery at your home altar with things that reflect the changeless nature of Jesus. Have each family member contribute to the gallery with an artwork, a musical piece, or something they wrote that reflects the changeless Jesus.

❧ Go on a family outing and photograph places in your community that are in stages of change. A "for sale" sign showing people changing their homes, a new building being constructed, and a tree with leaves falling off are examples of things you might photograph.

❧ Write a family prayer praising the changeless Christ and lifting up any fears of changes taking place in your lives.

Our Response to God's Grace

Dear Changeless Jesus, Changeless Christ,

When the world around us is changing so fast we sometimes get scared, please help us turn to You, knowing that Your love for us never changes. In Your love. Amen.

Ponderings

⤳ Write an essay examining the various changes that have taken place in your life, your feelings about those changes, and the role Christ played in your life during those times.

⤳ Study the following passages and write a description of the nature of the changeless God:

Psalm 90:1–2
Matthew 19:26
Psalm 139:1–4
Jeremiah 23:24
Leviticus 19:2
Deuteronomy 32:4
Psalm 145:13
Exodus 34:6–7
John 4:8

- Meditate on what the changeless nature of God means to you.
- How can the changeless anchor of God be an anchor in the lives of you and your children?
- How can you help your children draw upon God as a firm foundation in an ever-changing world?
- Commit anew to your role as spiritual leaders in your household. Examine how often you bring your family to worship among your community of faith. Do your children see you in Bible study and prayer? How might God strengthen you to be a model of one who holds firm to the changeless anchor of God?

Journal Jottings

Autumn Crop Walk

God's Grace to Us

Today's Reading: James 5:7–9

Be patient, then, brothers, until the Lord's coming. See how the farmer waits for the land to yield its valuable crop and how patient he is for the autumn and spring rains. James 5:7

Faith Walk

Walk along a country road or other place where crops are planted. What are the fields like? Are there still crops in the fields or have they all been harvested?

Faith Talk

✧ The farmer plants the seeds, nurtures them, and waits for the crops to mature. Growth does not happen overnight or even in a few days. It takes a whole season for the plants to mature. The farmer must be patient as he waits for the autumn harvest.

✧ We too must be patient as we wait for the Second Coming of Christ.

✧ Have you ever had to wait for something exciting to happen? Maybe you have had to wait for a birthday party, Christmas, or a vacation. The time seems endless. The hours and days drag by slowly. But finally the long-awaited event comes.

✧ As Christians we are waiting for the Second Coming of Christ. One day we will see Him return, and He will take us with Him to heaven where we will live forever at a party celebrating our Lord.

✧ For many Christians the wait for Christ's second return seems long. The hours and days tick by slowly. It is even harder because we do not know the day or hour in which Christ will return. But we have Jesus' promise that He *will* return. As we wait eagerly for Christ, we wait in hope.

Follow-up Activities

❧ Start an herb garden indoors. (Kits can be purchased from garden centers.) Practice patience as you eagerly wait for your herb garden to mature.

❧ Use an old tablecloth or sheet and markers to draw a mural of how you imagine heaven.

❧ Practice patience. Plan a special family outing a couple of weeks away.

❧ Silently watch sand run through an egg timer. When it is finished, let out a loud cheer. In the same way we wait for Christ and will rejoice at His return.

❧ Lie outside and watch the sky. Imagining what heaven is like. Remind one another that Christ will take all believers to heaven when He returns.

Our Response to God's Grace

Dear Christ, Lord of the Second Coming,

Please help us to be joyful at the hope of Your Second Coming, yet patient as we wait, knowing that You will return as You have promised. In Your name. Amen.

Ponderings

❧ Recall a time in your life when you struggled through pain and suffering. How could remembering the hope of eternal life we have through Jesus have helped you through this time?

❧ Read James 5:7–11. James was writing these words to people who were suffering at the hands of the rich. How can these words be a comfort to us?

❧ What promises does James hold out in these passages?

❧ Write out a description of your hope for eternal life.

❧ How can you hold out the hope of eternal life to others who are suffering?

Journal Jottings

Tied to Time

God's Grace to Us

Today's Reading: 2 Peter 3:8–9

But do not forget this one thing, dear friends: With the Lord a day is like a thousand years, and a thousand years are like a day. 2 Peter 3:8

Faith Walk

Take a walk in the evening, paying close attention to the changing length of days and the passing of time.

Faith Talk

✧ Discuss what determines the length of a day and a year and why the number of daylight hours changes.

✧ As winter gets closer and there are fewer daylight hours, how does the way we spend our time change?

✧ We live tied to time. We look at clocks to see if it is time to get up, to go to school, to eat a meal, or to go to an activity. Time affects everything we do.

✧ God does not live tied to time. It may seem that we must wait a long time for God's Second Coming. But to God it will seem as if only a moment has passed since He created the world.

✧ God is waiting for all who will come to faith so He can bring them into His kingdom.

Follow-up Activities

❋ Make a chart of the time of sunrise and sunset for two weeks. What do you see happening to the length of the days?

✤ Set a timer and sit for 10 minutes without talking or moving. After the timer beeps, discuss how it felt to wait that long. Sometimes time seems to move slowly, but we need every minute God gives us to share the Good News of Jesus.

✤ Pray each day during the next week for those who have not yet come to faith. Pray especially for those you know who do not yet have saving faith in Jesus.

✤ Check out a book from the library on time and learn about how people in different parts of the world and different historical eras have kept time.

✤ Count the clocks, watches, and other time-keeping devices in your home. What do they say about the importance of time in our lives? God's love is such that He isn't keeping time by hours or minutes. Instead, for God time is determined by whether all who will believe have come to faith.

Our Response to God's Grace

Dear Father, Creator of Time,

You do not keep time by days or hours but by the people who are yet to be saved. Please focus our hearts on those who need to know the way to heaven. Help us witness to them and, through the power of Your Spirit, bring them into Your kingdom. For Jesus' sake. Amen.

Ponderings

✐ Read Ecclesiastes 3:9–14. Verse 11 says, "He has also set eternity in the hearts of men." We are tied to time, yet time does not fulfill us because our souls were made immortal. God has set our hearts on eternity. Meditate on this concept and how it intersects with you.

✐ "I know that everything God does will endure forever" (verse 14). The works of God are permanent and changeless. How is that significant?

✐ Reread 2 Peter 3:8–9. Pay close attention to these words: "He is patient with you, not wanting anyone to perish, but everyone to come to repentance." God desires that all come to repentance and receive the forgiveness offered in Christ. At the final Judgment Day, He will judge all. Those who believe will be taken with Him to heaven. Those who do not repent and believe will be cast into eternal darkness. God's judgment will endure forever. For this reason God waits patiently for those who will turn to Him in faith and repentance.

✒ As we wait patiently for the Second Coming of the Lord, God has given us work to do. Read 2 Peter 3:10–15. How are we to live as we wait for the Lord's coming?

✒ Spend time praying, asking God for His wisdom, guidance, and power in helping you to live in these last days holy and blameless, bringing God's Gospel to others. Write three ways you can strive to carry out this commission in your life.

Journal Jottings

Treasure Hunt

God's Grace to Us

Today's Reading: Isaiah 33:5–6

He will be the sure foundation of your times, a rich store of salvation and wisdom and knowledge; the fear of the Lord is the key to this treasure. Isaiah 33:6

Faith Walk

Go on a treasure hunt. As you walk, look for "treasures"—beautiful leaves, interesting rocks, nutshells, or knobby sticks, anything you find that seems like a treasure from nature.

Faith Talk

✦ What is a treasure?

✦ What does the phrase "spiritual treasures" mean?

✦ What spiritual treasures does the Bible verse talk about?

✦ What do "salvation," "wisdom," and "knowledge" mean? Why are they treasures?

✦ How do we receive these treasures?

Follow-up Activities

❀ Set up a display of your treasures, for example trophies, jewelry, or photographs. Write a caption for each treasure, explaining why it is a treasure.

❀ Set up a display of the spiritual treasures God has given you, such as forgiveness, joy, and faith. Purchase some rhinestones and glue them to a piece of cardboard. Under each rhinestone write the name of a spiritual gift God has given you. For the rest of November use this display to help you pray prayers of thanksgiving.

* Have a "Secret Treasures" evening. Have each family member wrap up something that is a treasure to him or her. Take turns giving clues and trying to guess one another's treasures. Unwrap the treasures to see which guesses were correct. How can we "unwrap" the spiritual treasures God gives us?

* Be a secret treasure to someone outside your family. Some time during the next week, secretly do something kind for another person. For example, you might pick up trash in a neighbor's yard, return a runaway dog to its owner, or take someone's garbage can up to their house after the trash has been collected.

* Look up the words "treasure" and "treasures" in a Bible concordance. Read the passages you find. What do they teach us about spiritual treasures?

Our Response to God's Grace

Dear Triune God, Source of all Treasures,

Thank You for the treasures You have given us, especially the treasure of Your love. Please fill our lives with all spiritual treasures until they overflow into the lives of other people. In the name of our treasured Savior, Jesus. Amen.

Ponderings

* How has your faith been a treasure in your life? Write about it.

* The Bible verse says, "... the fear of the Lord is the key to this treasure." But how do we receive "the fear of the Lord?" In his book, *Celebration of Discipline*, Richard J. Foster talks about placing "ourselves before God so that He can transform us" and we can receive "the abundance of God." If we never attend church, surround ourselves with non-Christian friends, fail to pray or study God's Word, and fill our lives with nonspiritual media influences, we effectively shut our eyes to God's abundance in our lives. Instead, if, motivated by Christ's love, we seek to place ourselves in the church, in God's Word, and in prayer; our eyes will be opened to a greater abundance of God's grace.

❧ How is your life currently open to God's grace? Make a list of three ways you can seek God's guidance to improve on placing yourself where God is at work. Post the list in a prominent location and refer to it frequently.

❧ Keep a journal of how God blesses you with His treasures, His abundance. Use the journal also as a prayer journal. How has God blessed you with spiritual treasures? What is your thanksgiving response?

❧ The spiritual disciplines are not the balls and chains of law but a joyous journey to the treasures of God's abundance. Read more about this topic in Foster's book.

Journal Jottings

Praise-giving Walk

God's Grace to Us

Today's Reading: Nehemiah 9:5–6

"Stand up and praise the LORD your God, who is from everlasting to everlasting." Nehemiah 9:5b

Faith Walk

Take a walk in a place of your choice to look for God's wondrous nature in His creation. Praise Him for His marvelous deeds.

Faith Talk

✧ What is the difference between giving thanks to God and giving praise to God?

✧ What are some words people use to praise God?

✧ Brainstorm reasons for praising God.

✧ How can you praise God in your life?

✧ How can you add "praise giving" to your Thanksgiving?

Follow-up Activities

❧ Sing "Praise God from Whom All Blessings Flow" or another favorite hymn or song of praise.

❧ Write a psalm of praise and add it to your Thanksgiving worship.

❧ Draw names, keeping each one a secret. For a week, make a special effort to praise the person whose name you drew. Were you able to keep the secret and still praise one another? How do you think God might feel when we praise Him?

❧ Take turns bopping a balloon in the air. Each time you hit the balloon, yell out a word of praise to God.

❧ Memorize the Bible passage for the week. As you say it, use the following actions:

Stand up *(crouch low then jump up)*
And praise your God *(throw arms in air)*
Who is from everlasting to everlasting *(fling arms open wide)*
Nehemiah 9:5–6 *(hold out 9, 5, and 6 fingers on those numbers)*

Our Response to God's Grace

Dear Wondrous Heavenly Father,

We praise You for the marvelous things You have done in creating and taking care of your world. We especially praise You for Your love, through which You sacrificed Your Son Jesus on the cross so we might have eternal life. In His name. Amen.

Ponderings

↝ "No one who is born of God will continue to sin, because God's seed remains in him; he cannot go on sinning because he is born of God" (1 John 4:9).

Lord, the seed is planted in the earth and through Your goodness the earth produces bountiful riches. Your seed was planted in the woman and again in the hearts of all who believe, and the harvest is life and righteousness. We praise You for Your seed!

↝ "Whoever believes in Me, as the Scripture has said, streams of living water will flow from within him" (John 7:38).

The seeds are watered with the water of life; for out of the dead seed will grow a new life. You bring forth the waters that produce vegetation and the water that gives us a new life in Christ. You pour Your Spirit upon us so the waters may pour from us. We praise You for water!

⨍ "A shoot will come up from the stump of Jesse; from his roots a branch will bear its fruit" (Isaiah 11:1).

The seed takes root and a shoot grows. Christ, You are the Root of Jesse, the Shoot that produces fruit. We are the fruit. We praise You, the Root in which we are grounded and from which we receive life.

⨍ "Then another angel came out of the temple and called in a loud voice to him who was sitting on the cloud, 'Take your sickle and reap, for the time to reap has come, for the harvest of the earth is right'" (Revelations 14:15).

You are the Lord of the harvest. From You comes all the abundance of produce that we receive. You are also the Lord who will harvest souls on Judgment Day. You will separate the wheat from the chaff, throwing the chaff into the fire and bringing the wheat into the heavenly storehouse. We praise You for the abundant harvest and for Your goodness and mercy!

⨍ "Then Jesus declared, 'I am the Bread of Life. He who comes to Me will never be hungry, and he who believes in Me will never be thirsty'" (John 6:35).

Bread is a gift from You, O Lord. Just as bread nurtures our body, You nurture our soul, giving it every good thing that it needs so we may never again be hungry. For the bread of life, we praise You, O Christ!

Journal Jottings

Thanksgiving Walk

God's Grace to Us

Today's Reading: Psalm 95:1–7

Let us come before Him with thanksgiving and extol Him with music and song. Psalm 95:2

Faith Walk

As you take a walk around your neighborhood, seek things for which to thank God. When you find something, stop and say a quick prayer of thanks.

Faith Talk

✧ What are the things you are most thankful for in your life?

✧ How are all things a gift from God?

✧ In the Bible verses, what is the psalmist thankful for?

✧ How can you show more thankfulness in your lives?

✧ Ask the Lord to give you hearts of thankfulness.

Follow-up Activities

❧ Write a family psalm of thanksgiving and use it at your Thanksgiving meal.

❧ Write the words "We are thankful for ..." on a large sheet of paper and tape it on the wall near your family altar. As family members think of things for which they are thankful, write or draw them on the banner.

❧ Make name cards for your Thanksgiving celebration. Fold index cards in half. On one side write the names of guests and decorate with Thanksgiving stickers. On the other side write, "Something I am thankful for is ..." At your Thanksgiving feast place pencils and name cards at each spot. Give everyone time to finish the sentence. Before starting the meal, pray a Thanksgiving prayer, then go around the table and have each person read their card.

❧ Sing a favorite Thanksgiving hymn.

❧ Make a circle. Have each family member throw a beanbag in the air as they say what they are thankful for. Then catch the beanbag and pass it to the next person.

Our Response to God's Grace

Dear Father, Abundant Giver,

You have blessed us with many gifts. For this we thank You. We ask You for yet one more gift—the gift of a thankful heart. In the abundance of Christ's love we pray. Amen.

Ponderings

❧ "Sing, O Daughter of Zion; shout aloud, O Israel!" (Zephaniah 3:14a). Lift up an offering of Thanksgiving with your voice;—pray, sing, praise, and witness God's goodness in your life. Shout it aloud!

❧ "Be glad and rejoice with all your heart, O Daughter of Jerusalem!" (Zephaniah 3:14b). What blessings does your heart have to be thankful for? Lift them up to the Lord by offering Him a thankful heart.

❧ "Therefore, I urge you, brothers, in view of God's mercy, to offer your bodies as living sacrifices, holy and pleasing to God—this is your spiritual act of worship" (Romans 12:1). Lift up an offering of thanksgiving with your body; live a life pleasing to God, extend God's blessings to others by serving them, fold your hands in prayer and lift and clap your hands in praise. Let all that you do with your body be a gift of thanksgiving for what God has done for you, through Jesus.

❧ "From what you have, take an offering for the LORD" (Exodus 35:5a). "All who are skilled among you are to come and make everything the LORD has commanded" (Exodus 35:10). Lift up an offering of thanksgiving with your time, talents, and treasures.

➷ "When anyone is guilty in any of these ways, he must confess in what way he has sinned" (Leviticus 5:5). Lift up, as an offering of thanksgiving, your sins. For the grace we receive through Christ's blood is the greatest gift for which to be thankful. So confess your sins in thanksgiving for the resurrected Lord and receive the abundant gift of His grace.

Journal Jottings

December

Pointing Ahead to Christ

God's Grace to Us

Today's Reading: Luke 1:26–38

[The angel said,] "You will be with child and give birth to a son, and you are to give Him the name Jesus. He will be great and will be called the Son of the Most High. The Lord God will give Him the throne of His father David, and He will reign over the house of Jacob forever; His kingdom will have no end." Luke 1:31–33

Faith Walk

Look for signs of Christmas as you walk around your neighborhood. Which ones point to the coming Christ Child? Which ones point away from Him?

Faith Talk

✦ Advent is from a Latin word that means "coming."

✦ During Advent we look forward to the birth of Jesus, salvation, and the coming of eternal life. We focus on His coming to earth as a baby and His return when He will come to earth again some day.

✦ In the Bible verse it tells us that Jesus will be given the throne—He will reign (rule) and His kingdom will never end.

✦ What kind of king was Jesus sent to be?

✦ How can you, during Advent, look forward to Jesus' coming?

Follow-up Activities

❀ As you decorate your house for Christmas, look for things that point to Christ. For example, point out the star at the top of the tree and see who can tell the story of the Wise Men, or compare your evergreen tree to the gift of everlasting life.

❦ Make Advent cards that point ahead to Jesus. The inside message could read "Coming soon: Baby Jesus!" or "A King will be born." Or add any Advent message you create. Give the cards away.

❦ Trumpets will announce the second coming of Christ. Purchase inexpensive trumpet ornaments at a craft store. Hot glue them to a decorative string to make a garland to drape over your home altar.

❦ Create a simple Advent calendar to help you count the days until Christmas. Cut a cross from cardboard as a reminder that Jesus came to be our Savior. Glue on one "jewel"—decorative rocks, sequins, or cake decorations—for every day from now until Christmas. The jewels help us remember the coming of Christ the King and His heavenly kingdom. Remove one jewel each day. When the last jewel is gone, it is Christmas!

❦ Set a goal to attend every Advent worship service. Attend other Christ-centered Christmas events in your community, such as a concert or live nativity. Think of each service and event as a party for the coming King.

Our Response to God's Grace

Dear Heavenly Father,

As we wait for Christmas, renew Your Spirit within us to keep our eyes focused on the coming of Jesus, the Savior of the world. Give us patience as we wait excitedly for His Second Coming. In the name of Christ, our King. Amen.

Ponderings

☙ When life gets stressful or painful, we can cling to the knowledge that Christ came to bring us salvation and to the hope that He will return. What does this knowledge and hope mean for you?

☙ The holiday season is often hectic and stressful. Go for a walk alone to refuel. In the quietness, pray for the Holy Spirit to fill your heart with Christ.

☞ Do your holiday activities reflect Christ or are they merely busy activities? Reduce holiday stress by weeding out the less meaningful secular activities. Center your holiday preparations on the spiritual richness of Christ.

☞ Read Luke 1:46–56. These words record Mary's song of praise as she prepared for Christ's birth. Write your own prayer of praise for God's gifts in your life—especially the gift of His Son.

☞ The Old Testament is filled with prophecies of Christ. Read the following verses from Isaiah and use them to meditate on the kingdom of Christ: 7:14, 9:1–7, 11:1–16, 16:5, 42:1–4, 52:13–53:12, 60:1–3, 60:6, 61:1–3.

☞ What has God provided for us through Christ?

Journal Jottings

Santa Claus Seek (December 6)

God's Grace to Us

Today's Reading: John 3:16–21

For God so loved the world that He gave His one and only Son, that whoever believes in Him shall not perish but have eternal life. John 3:16

Faith Walk

Take a walk around your neighborhood. Count the number of Santas you find. Count the number of nativity sets.

Faith Talk

✧ Santa Claus, or Saint Nicholas, is based upon the story of a priest who secretly gave gifts of money to poor people hundreds of years ago. We observe St. Nicholas Day on December 6.

✧ St. Nicholas gave gifts in secret. He wanted people to focus on the gift and not who gave it. How can we secretly give gifts at Christmas?

✧ Read the verse at the beginning of this devotion. What is the greatest gift? Why is this gift the greatest of all?

✧ How can we keep Christmas focused on Jesus instead of Santa Claus?

Follow-up Activities

❧ Place a Santa Claus facing a crèche (nativity) in your home. Talk about the real St. Nicholas who worshiped the Christ Child.

❧ Make a donation to a family or an organization serving families in need.

❧ Make a "Baby Jesus in a Box":

1. Decorate a small box to look like a gift.

2. Glue yellow yarn in the bottom of the box to resemble straw.

3. Wrap a 3" square of cloth around a round wooden clothespin to look like a baby.

4. Draw a face on the clothespin.

5. Lay baby Jesus in the "manger."

♣ Check out a book on saints from your local library. Read about the different saints. Talk about how we are all saints because Christ came to bring us forgiveness!

♣ Make a sign that says, "Jesus—the real gift of Christmas!" Hang your sign in a window.

Our Response to God's Grace

Dear God, Gracious Heavenly Father,

Your Christmas gift to us was Your Son and the eternal life He gives. Help us to keep that as the center of our Christmas and to share Your gift with others. In the name of Jesus. Amen.

Ponderings

☞ Read Ephesians 2:8–9. Can we do anything to earn the gift of salvation? Reflect on the phrases "by grace," "through faith," "gift of God," and "not by works." Look at your life. Do you try to earn God's favor? If a person, out of love, presents a gift to another person and the receiver tries to pay for it, it cheapens both their relationship and the gift. In the same way, God has presented a gift of love to us—salvation—which is priceless. By trying to earn it, we reject God's gift, denying our helplessness and cutting ourselves off from God.

☞ If we do not do good works to earn salvation, why do we do good works at all? Read and meditate on Galatians 5:13, Ephesians 2:10, 1 Corinthians 10:31, and 1 John 4:15–5:5. Consider this definition of good works from *Luther's*

Small Catechism: "In God's sight a good work is everything that a child of God does, speaks, or thinks in faith according to the Ten Commandments, for the glory of God, and for the benefit of his or her neighbor." Ask yourself the question again. Write your thoughts on paper.

✎ What role do gifts play in your home during the holidays? How could your gifts better reflect Christ's gift of salvation?

✎ Salvation comes through the forgiveness offered in Christ. Forgiveness heals our relationship with God, which was broken by sin. Apply this to your relationship with your children. How can forgiveness change your relationships? What about relationships outside the home?

✎ Read Romans 12:6–8. What gifts has God given you? How can you use them to build up your family? God's kingdom?

Journal Jottings

Snow Angels

God's Grace to Us

Today's Reading: Luke 1:26–38

But the angel said to her, "Do not be afraid, Mary, you have found favor with God. You will be with child and give birth to a son, and you are to give Him the name Jesus." Luke 1:30–31

Faith Walk

Walk until you find a clean patch of snow. Lie down and make snow angels. If there is no snow where you live, find a patch of concrete. Take turns tracing one another with sidewalk chalk. Make the arms look like wings and the legs look like a robe.

Faith Talk

✢ What role did the angel play in today's Bible reading?

✢ What message did the angel bring? To whom did he bring this message?

✢ Read another part of the Christmas story in Luke 2:8–20. What role did the angels play here?

✢ There are lots of stories about angels today. But some people get so excited about angels they forget about God. We need to remember that angels, like us, are not God. They are servants of God, witnessing Him, praising Him, and doing His work.

✢ How can you be a messenger for God?

Follow-up Activities

❧ Be a messenger of God's love—donate a Christmas storybook to your library.

✤ Be a messenger of God's love—get some tracts from your local Christian bookstore and leave them at a public place, such as a rest stop or with your tip at a restaurant.

✤ Be a messenger of God's love—write out your favorite Bible verses and post them around your home to remind one another of God's love.

✤ Be a messenger of God's love—give up eating out or going to a movie and use the money to support a missionary.

✤ Thank God for His messengers of love that tell the Good News of Jesus—the angels and prophets, pastors and teachers, and one another.

Our Response to God's Grace

Dear Heavenly Father,

Thank You for sending the angels at Christmas to spread the joyous message of salvation. Help us to spread this wondrous message to others. For Jesus' sake. Amen.

Ponderings

✐ What messengers of God's love has God placed in your life? Your pastor, your parents, your spouse? What makes these messengers effective?

✐ How can you be a messenger of God's love to your children? To others? How can you improve your ability to communicate God's love to others? Ask for God's help.

✐ Read these Bible passages about angels:

Exodus 23:20
Luke 22:39–46
Matthew 28:1–10
Psalm 91:11–12
Matthew 18:10
Hebrews 1:1–14
Matthew 13:49–50

What are the roles of angels in these passages?

🖋 What is the purpose of God's creation? Read Revelation 5:13–14.

🖋 Read Ephesians 4:11–13. Ask yourself, "What gifts has God blessed me with that I can use to build up His kingdom?"

🖋 God clearly brings the message of His love to us through His Word, the waters of Baptism, and His body and blood—given and poured out for the forgiveness of sins. How often do you come into His presence to receive these gifts of His grace?

Journal Jottings

Quiet Christmas

God's Grace to Us

Today's Reading: Luke 2:1–7

And she gave birth to her firstborn, a son. She wrapped Him in cloths and placed Him in a manger, because there was no room for them in the inn. Luke 2:7

Faith Walk

Take a walk at night or in the early morning when few people are around. Stop. Stand very still. What sounds do you hear amidst the quietness? Imagine the cries of a newborn baby breaking the silence of a certain quiet night.

Faith Talk

✧ Jesus, the King of kings, came into the world quietly, without the fanfare of a royal court. He was born in a stable and laid in a manger, a feeding trough for animals.

✧ Jesus' parents were poor in money but humble and rich in faith. Why do you think God chose to send Jesus to be born into this family instead of a rich family, a royal family?

✧ God wants us to have faith. That means He wants us to believe without seeing. Would it take more faith to believe that Jesus is the King of kings if He was born into a poor family or into a royal family?

✧ What can you do to quietly celebrate Christmas?

Follow-up Activities

❧ Set a timer for 2–3 minutes. Hold hands in a circle. Pray silently. When the timer rings, quietly hug one another and walk away.

✤ Jesus came into the world to be a servant. His greatest act of service was to die on the cross for us. In love we want to serve Him back. Read Matthew 25:40 and plan a family servant event. Ideas could include cleaning the church for Christmas, volunteering at a soup kitchen, or collecting items for a gift drive.

✤ Turn off the television, radios, and computers for a day and spend the day talking in hushed voices. At the end of the day, ask God to help you treat one another with quiet love.

✤ Listen to an instrumental Christmas CD or cassette. What pictures of Christmas do you see in your mind? Where is Christ in those pictures?

✤ Draw names from a hat. Be a Secret Pal to that person until Christmas. Do special things to show one another God's love.

Our Response to God's Grace

Dear Jesus, King of kings,

You came into the world quietly. Few people knew or even cared who You were. Yet You are the greatest gift this world has ever received. Open the eyes of all to see that You are our Savior King. Amen.

Ponderings

✐ Read Isaiah 30:15. It is hard to find quietness in the busy rush of Christmas. Pray for God's help in finding a quiet spot in your soul and find time in your day to reflect on His Word. Plan to come early the next time you worship. Sit quietly and reflect on the symbols of His love that surround you.

✐ Christ's blessed entry into this world was almost unnoticed. Look for the blessings God has placed in your life that go almost unnoticed. Thank Him for those gifts.

✐ Find one person who needs to be uplifted and, without drawing attention to yourself, do something to raise that person's spirits. Thank God for the opportunity to share His love with others.

✑ Memorize the verse at the beginning of this devotion. Carry it in your head and heart and reflect on its meaning as you worship the Christ Child.

✑ How many ways can you worship Christ this Christmas?

Journal Jottings

Noisy Christmas

God's Grace to Us

Today's Reading: Luke 2:8–20

Suddenly a great company of the heavenly host appeared with the angel, praising God and saying, "Glory to God in the highest, and on earth peace to men on whom His favor rests." Luke 2:13–14

Faith Walk

Walk to a busy holiday area such as a shopping center, a downtown, a mall, or a holiday display. Can you pick out any noises that celebrate the birth of the Christ Child? What noises celebrate secular things?

Faith Talk

✧ Reread Luke 2. How many noises can you think of that celebrated the birth of Jesus?

✧ God sent people, angels, animals, and a star to celebrate Jesus' birth.

✧ God celebrated Jesus' birth with music, words, offerings, light, and prayer.

✧ What Christmas celebrations forget the birth of Jesus? What Christmas celebrations remember the birth of Jesus?

✧ What can you do to celebrate the birth of Jesus with joyous music?

Follow-up Activities

❧ Christmas is the day we celebrate the birthday of Jesus. Have a birthday party for Jesus.

❧ Write a family celebration cheer to rejoice that Christ has come.

❀ Sing "Joy to the World."

❀ Tell the Christmas story and record it. Send the recording to a family member who lives far away.

❀ Go Christmas caroling at a nursing home. Share a Christmas hug with the residents.

Our Response to God's Grace

Dear God the Father Almighty, Maker of Heaven and Earth,

You used Your creation to announce and celebrate the birth of Your Son. Send Your Holy Spirit to create in our hearts and our home a spirit of celebration and joy at the birth of Your Son. In the name of Your Son, our Savior. Amen.

Ponderings

✒ Imagine you are a shepherd listening to the angels, then going to worship Jesus. How would this change your life?

✒ Which Christmas song has the most meaning for you? Why?

✒ Long before Christ was born, He was proclaimed and prophesied. Read Isaiah 9:6–7. What characteristics of Christ are proclaimed in these verses?

✒ Listen to what comes out of your mouth during the course of your day. Do your words and attitudes proclaim your relationship with Christ or your sinful nature? Ask for forgiveness through Christ for the times you fail. And ask for God's help in proclaiming Christ in your words and actions.

✒ Read 1 Chronicles 16:8–36. Divide a sheet of paper in half. On one side write "God's Love." On the other side write "My Response." Reread the Bible passage. Under "God's Love" write the ways God reaches out to you in love. Under "My Response" write the ways He helps you celebrate and respond to His love. God's relationship with us is the greatest love story ever.

Journal Jottings

Good-bye? Christmas

God's Grace to Us

Today's Reading: Luke 2:17–20

But Mary treasured up all these things and pondered them in her heart. Luke 2:19

Faith Walk

Several days after Christmas take an evening walk around your neighborhood. How many Christmas decorations have already been put away? How many lights are off?

Faith Talk

✧ Is Christmas Day a "good-bye" to Christmas or a "hello"?

✧ Most people do their Christmas celebrating before and on Christmas Day. For many the holiday ends the day after Christmas. But for Christians, the true Christmas holiday begins *on* Christmas because our long-awaited Savior has come. Celebrate!

✧ You often hear stories and songs about the "Twelve Days of Christmas." Did you know that the 12 days of Christmas end on Epiphany (January 6)—the day we celebrate how the Wise Men came to worship Jesus? How can you continue to celebrate Christmas?

✧ Mary "treasured" and "pondered" the Christmas events. How can you treasure and ponder them?

✧ When does the Christmas season end for you?

Follow-up Activities

✤ Celebrate Christmas by taking an elderly widow or widower out to eat.

✤ Make "It's a boy!" cards to send to people, announcing the birth of Christ.

✤ Host a baby shower. Deliver the gifts to a shelter, crisis pregnancy center, or other agency to help remember the birth of Christ.

✤ Act out the Christmas story.

✤ Make a treasure box of Christmas memories to help you treasure and ponder the Christmas events.

Our Response to God's Grace

Dear Christ,

Please help us "treasure" and "ponder" the Christmas story as we celebrate Your birth. In Your treasured name. Amen.

Ponderings

✐ A virgin birth. Visiting shepherds. Reports of an angel choir. Luke 2:18 says, "and all who heard it were amazed at what the shepherds said to them." Surprise, astonishment, maybe even disbelief—how would you have reacted? Mary's reaction was to "treasure" the story unfolding before her, "ponder" its implications, and "store" it in the safekeeping of her heart, her soul. What is your reaction to the Christmas story?

✐ John 1:1–18 reports a very different version of Christ who came at Christmas. What does this passage tell us about Jesus' entry into the world? About Jesus?

✐ Jesus' birth is not the end of the holidays, but the beginning of the unfolding of God's glorious plan of salvation. Read some other biblical beginnings:

Genesis 1:1–2:3

Genesis 3:20

Genesis 12:1–3

Acts 2:1–4

Who is at the center of all these beginnings?

⤳ Think back to the beginnings and endings in your life. Who was at the center of them?

⤳ Life is full of beginnings—births, baptisms, weddings, new days, new years, and new jobs. And life is full of endings—deaths, divorces, graduations, children moving away, retirements, evening shadows, falling leaves, and New Year's Eve. With each beginning and ending come challenges, such as joy, sadness, guilt, relief, hopes, fears, laughter, and tears. Each challenge can draw us closer to the Lord because He will never leave us empty. Seek His comfort, promises, and guidance in His Holy Scriptures, touch Him through the wine and the bread, pour out your tears and laughter to Him in prayer, and ultimately cling to the baby, the cross, and the gift of eternal life.

Journal Jottings

Through the Year

Light of the World

God's Grace to Us

Today's Reading: John 8:12

[Jesus said,] "I am the Light of the world. Whoever follows Me will never walk in darkness, but will have the light of life." John 8:12

Faith Walk

Walk to a dark area. Take along various sources of light, such as a flashlight, a penlight, a lantern, a match, a candle, and a lighter. Which one pierces the darkness the best?

Faith Talk

✧ Jesus is our Light.

✧ Jesus lights the way to heaven. We call the world *dark* because it is filled with sin. We call Jesus the *Light* because He breaks through the darkness of sin by His death and resurrection. He shows us that through faith in Him as our Savior, we can be alive eternally (forever) with Him.

✧ How can Jesus be a light every day in our lives?

✧ How can we help to bring the light of Jesus to others?

Follow-up Activities

❧ Hunt for all the sources of light in your home. Which is brightest? Which is dimmest?

❧ Shine a flashlight in the darkest corners of your home. What did you find? We were born into the darkness of sin, but sinless Jesus pierces our darkness with forgiveness.

❧ Sing "This Little Gospel Light of Mine" (found in *Little Ones Sing Praise*, Concordia Publishing House, 1989).

❧ Be a light to another person. Do an act of love to someone who is hurting.

❧ We light the candles in church to remind us that Jesus is present as the Light of the world. Light a candle at mealtime to help you remember that Jesus is always present in your home.

Our Response to God's Grace

Dear Christ, Light of the World,

*   Wash away the darkness of our sin and light the way to heaven. Help us to be a light to others by telling them of the freedom from sin that can be found in You. In Your light we pray. Amen.*

Ponderings

✐ What were the darkest days of your life? Where was Christ in those days?

✐ What role does the light of Jesus play in your daily life?

✐ Light illuminates. In the same way, God's Word illuminates His Spirit. Make a commitment to study God's Word daily. Live in the confidence of your baptismal vows as you receive the forgiveness that is yours because Christ has pierced through the darkness of sin.

✐ Meditate on the light of Christ in this world and in the world to come.

✐ Make a commitment to share Christ's light with another person by witnessing your faith.

Journal Jottings

Alpha and Omega Hike

God's Grace to Us

Today's Reading: Revelation 22:12–16

"I am the Alpha and the Omega, the First and the Last, the Beginning and the End." Revelation 22:13

Faith Walk

Hike a trail that ends at the same place it started. Before the hike, mark the starting point with a stick. At the end of the hike say, "This stick marks where we began and ended." Then ask, "How do we find the beginning and end of a circle?" Talk about the answers and ideas as you return home.

Faith Talk

✧ In the book of Revelation, Jesus calls Himself "the Alpha and the Omega." The alpha and the omega are the first and last letters of the Greek alphabet. Jesus was calling Himself the First and the Last. He was saying that He has no beginning and no end. He rules over all of human time.

✧ Jesus was with the Father in the beginning and will be with Him throughout eternity. He is eternal, forever—like a circle, with no beginning and no end.

✧ We know that only God can exist with no beginning and no end. We also know Jesus has no beginning or end. Therefore, what do we know about Jesus?

✧ Read the entire Bible selection. What do you think Jesus means when He says, "I am the Root, the Offspring of David, and the bright Morning Star" (Revelation 22:16)?

✧ What does Jesus promise to all who believe?

Follow-up Activities

♣ Our time is limited. Make a timeline of your life so far. Where have you seen Jesus along the way?

♣ The earth's time is limited. Use your Bible and resources from the library to make a timeline of world history, focusing on God's role in the world. For younger children, keep the timeline simple.

♣ God is timeless. Arrange two mirrors so your reflection seems to go on forever in both directions. Your reflection is an optical illusion—God is not. His past has no beginning and His future has no end.

♣ Have a circle-hunt competition. Give each person a bag and set a timer for five minutes. Who can find the most circle things to place in their bag during the five minutes?

♣ On a large sheet of paper write "Alpha" and "Omega" in bubble letters. Brainstorm names for Jesus and write them in the bubble letters. Display your finished banner in a prominent location.

Our Response to God's Grace

Dear Heavenly Father,

We cannot understand eternity or forever, yet You are eternal. You have always been and always will be. Give us faith to believe that which we cannot understand. In the name of Your eternal Son. Amen.

Ponderings

✐ Read Exodus 3:13–16. God says, "I AM WHO I AM" and "I AM has sent me to you." What is God's name, His nature? I AM.

✐ In Revelation 22:12, Jesus says, "I AM coming soon." In verse 13, He says, "I AM the Alpha and the Omega." And again in verse 16, He says, "I AM the Root and the Offspring of David, the bright Morning Star." What do you think Jesus is saying about who He is in these Bible passages within the context of Exodus 3:13–16?

✎ Alpha and Omega. First and Last. Beginning and End. Eternal. God was from infinity and He will go into infinity. God was and is forever. There is no "before God." Read Psalm 90:1–4.

✎ In Revelation 22:13, Jesus says, "I am the Alpha and the Omega, the First and the Last, the Beginning and the End." Who is Jesus again proclaiming He is?

✎ Jesus says, "I am the Root and the Offspring of David, and the bright Morning Star" (Revelation 22:16). Here Jesus establishes Himself as the Messiah. Why does Jesus so carefully, in this passage, establish Himself as God and the Messiah? Why must His authority be established?

Journal Jottings

Never-Ending Prayer

God's Grace to Us

Today's Reading: 1 Thessalonians 5:12–28

Be joyful always; pray continually; give thanks in all circumstances, for this is God's will for you in Christ Jesus. 1 Thessalonians 5:16–18

Faith Walk

Take a prayer walk. Begin the walk with a prayer, asking God to open your eyes and heart to see those things for which you can pray. During the walk, look for reasons to stop and say a prayer. As you walk past a home where you know there are needs, such as someone who is sick or a family without faith, pray for God's presence in that home. When you see a beautiful flower garden, give a prayer of thanksgiving. As you see someone driving or riding in a car, pray for safe travel. When your walk is finished, ask God to help you pray continuously.

Faith Talk

✧ When does God want us to pray?

✧ Why does God want us to pray continuously?

✧ Brainstorm a list of different types of prayers, different times to pray, and different things to pray for.

✧ What does the Bible verse mean, "give thanks in all circumstances?"

✧ The Bible verse ends "for that is God's will for you in Christ Jesus." What difference does Christ Jesus make in your everyday life? How does He make a difference in our prayer life?

Follow-up Activities

✤ Praying continuously is a discipline—it takes work. Support one another in this effort. Spend some time in the evening talking about where, when, and how you prayed that day.

✤ Learn some prayers you can say together (see Appendix A).

✤ Write a list of different types of prayers, such as memorized prayers, requests, or prayers of praise. Post it in a prominent location as a reminder to pray continuously.

✤ Make prayer pillowcases. Use fabric paint to write the words "Pray continuously" on pillowcases and decorate with pictures of people for whom you can pray, things for which you are thankful, words of praise to God, and other prayer ideas.

✤ Write the Bible passage on an index card and carry it for a week as a reminder to pray continuously.

✤ If you have not already started a prayer journal, do so now. As you think of things to pray for, write them in the journal. Use the journal for prayer ideas during devotions. Occasionally reread the journal and think about how God answered your prayers.

Our Response to God's Grace

Dear God, Father in Heaven,

Because of what Christ has done for us, we can always come to You in prayer. In fact, it is Your will that we pray without stopping. Help us to do so. In His name we pray. Amen.

Ponderings

🖎 Read Galatians 4:6 and Philippians 4:6–7. Through Baptism we are in Christ Jesus. And the Spirit of Christ Jesus dwelling in us cries out "Abba, Father." Because we have the Spirit of God in us, we too call out to our Father and receive His peace, a peace beyond understanding that guards our hearts and minds.

꙾ Read John 15:7. Christ dwells in us and we listen to Him. He opens to us God's heart and we pray as if in one voice with God. Through our prayers we receive comfort and strength that comes from knowing our heavenly Father hears us and responds with His love and grace.

꙾ Write a description of the role prayer has played in your life. How, through the power of the Spirit, can you improve your prayer life?

꙾ Receive strength for your prayer life through a prayer partner, a person with whom you can pray and share your prayer needs. Ask God to guide you to a spiritually mature person who can be your prayer partner.

Journal Jottings

Rock Solid

God's Grace to Us

Today's Reading: 2 Samuel 22:1–4

"The Lord is my rock, my fortress, and my deliverer." 2 Samuel 22:2

Faith Walk

Look for different kinds of rocks in your neighborhood, such as boulders, stones, and pebbles. How many kinds of rocks can you find?

Faith Talk

✧ Think of as many words as possible to describe a rock. How is God like a rock?

✧ How has God been a rock in your life?

✧ In the Bible passage, David praises God for saving him from the hand of Saul, who was trying to kill David. David calls God his Rock, his Fortress, and his Deliverer.

✧ David leaned on the strength of God in times of trouble. What troubled times have you had? Do you think you leaned on the strength of God? How did you lean on God or depend on His strength?

✧ When our feet are firmly planted on God, our Rock, we will not crash down in the storms of life.

Follow-up Activities

❋ Glue a small pebble to the center of an 18-inch string and tie the ends of the string into a necklace. Wear it as a reminder that God is our Rock.

❋ Cut gray construction paper into rock shapes. Write the Bible passage on the paper rocks and display them around the house.

❧ Sing a song that reminds you of God's strength, such as "God Is Bigger Than the Boogey Man" (Veggie Tales) or "My God Is So Big" (available in *Little Ones Sing Praise*, Concordia Publishing House, 1989).

❧ Start a rock collection. Go to a toy, discount, or craft store and buy a kit for polishing rocks. Look up several Bible passages about rocks (use your Bible concordance), write them on paper, and display them with your rock collection.

❧ Write a list of different words for "rock." Say the Bible verse substituting those words for rock. Which words work? Which don't? Why?

Our Response to God's Grace

Dear God our Father, our Rock, and our Strength,

Please help us to plant our feet on You so we don't blow over in the storms of life. Through Jesus our Rock, we pray. Amen.

Ponderings

☞ *God is my Rock.* When I fear that the storms of life will overtake me and I will drown in my problems, God holds me up. *On Him I lean.*

☞ *God is my Rock.* When I am tired and weary from life and I have no strength left in me, God is there beside me, holding me up so I do not fall. *In Him I find strength.*

☞ *God is my Rock.* When the world seems like shifting sand, with no firm foundation on which to plant my feet, I can plant my feet on God, my Rock. *He is my constant and ever sure foundation.*

☞ *God is my Rock.* When I feel alone in my role as a parent, trying to impart values and faith to my children, God is by my side. *He walks with me and shows me that He is the Way.*

☞ *God is my Rock, my Strength, my Sure Foundation, and my Salvation. With Him I shall stand firm to the end.*

Journal Jottings

Step on a Crack

God's Grace to Us

Today's Reading: Romans 6:15–23

For the wages of sin is death, but the gift of God is eternal life in Christ Jesus our Lord. Romans 6:23

Faith Walk

Take a walk on a sidewalk, but try not to step on any cracks. Recall the children's game: "Step on a crack and you'll break your mother's back." Do you have stories to tell about playing this game?

Faith Talk

✧ The children's game, "Step on a crack and you'll break your mother's back," leaves no room for mistakes. We know that Mom's back won't really be broken, but we pretend that it takes only one mistake—stepping on one crack—for that to happen. God's Law is even more strict. All it takes is one time to break God's Law and we deserve the punishment. What is the punishment? Eternal death and damnation.

✧ It is impossible for us to keep God's Law. The Bible tells us, "All have sinned and fallen short of the glory of God" (Romans 3:23).

✧ But God has not left us to die under the Law. He sent Jesus to live a perfect life without sin. He lived a perfect life, then took the punishment for our sins when He died on the cross. He did this to free us from sin and the power of the Law. Jesus died so we could be forgiven. We are now sinless in God's eyes.

✧ Through Jesus, all who believe are made righteous and receive eternal life.

✧ Now we try to keep the Law, not to save ourselves, but to show God that we love Him because He saved us.

Follow-up Activities

✤ Act out a situation where one person is the judge and another is being judged. What did that person do wrong? What sentence did the judge hand down?

✤ Now pretend that someone comes into the same situation and offers to take the punishment. How does that feel?

✤ Sing "Amazing Grace" or another hymn or song that teaches about God's grace to us.

✤ Play "Simon Says." If you make one mistake, you're out. In the same way, because of our sin, we deserve to be out of God's family. But thanks be to Jesus for dying on the cross so we can be part of God's family!

✤ Cut a piece of paper into the shape of stone tablets. Write the Ten Commandments on the tablet (see Appendix B). See Exodus 20:1–20 or *Luther's Small Catechism* for a list of the commandments. Post the Ten Commandments on your refrigerator. At the very bottom of the paper add this Bible verse: "This is love for God: to obey His commands." 1 John 5:3a.

This is love for God: to obey His commands

Our Response to God's Grace

Dear Father, Righteous Judge,

We cannot keep Your law perfectly. We are guilty of sin and deserve death. But because Jesus died for our sins, we are forgiven and receive heaven. Thank You for Your loving grace. Help us to love You in return and keep Your commandments. In the name of Jesus who saves us. Amen.

Ponderings

✐ *Step on a crack ...* Adam and Eve stepped on the crack when they disobeyed God and ate the fruit from the tree. Like Pandora's Box, the door to sin was opened. The genetic code of humankind and of all of God's creation was forever changed. Evil, sin, and all vileness had entered the world.

❧ *... And you'll break your mother's back.* After just one sin, the consequence was death. One sin and all was made evil, abhorrent to God. Psalm 11:20 says, "The LORD detests a man of perverse heart but He delights in those whose ways are blameless." Because every person is sinful by nature, God, who is perfect and righteous, cannot bear us; therefore, we must be cast into the outer darkness. We are broken.

❧ *But the crack is gone ...* God in His loving nature did not leave us to despair. He made us righteous and holy through Christ. "This is love: not that we loved God, but that He loved us and sent His Son as an atoning sacrifice for our sins" (1 John 4:10). Jesus' blood washed away our sins. We are made perfect.

❧ *The punishment is lifted ...* Instead of eternal death, we now receive eternal life!

❧ *We are free to walk righteously ...* Now we no longer live in fear of stepping on a crack. Instead, we come to receive His forgiveness in His body and blood. We walk hand-in-hand with the Lord, who guides our steps and helps us respond to Him in loving obedience.

Journal Jottings

Ready ... Set ... Go ... Race!

God's Grace to Us

Today's Reading: 2 Timothy 4:6–8

I have fought the good fight, I have finished the race, I have kept the faith. 2 Timothy 4:7

Faith Walk

Have a race in a safe spot through your neighborhood or around your house. Give the less capable runners a lead. Who won?

Faith Talk

✧ Paul compares keeping the Christian faith to running a race. How are they the same?

✧ What kinds of "training" do people use to become better runners? What kinds of things help us to "train" in keeping the faith? Where is the finish line in our race of keeping the faith?

✧ The best thing about the "faith race" is that we do not win by being first. Instead, Jesus has already won the prize for us. We win our race by being steady and holding on to our faith until the end. All who stand firm in their faith until they die are winners. Read 2 Timothy 4:7 again. What is the prize? Now read 2 Timothy 4:8. What does "the crown of righteousness" mean?

Follow-up Activities

❦ Have a family track meet. Try different kinds of races—a wheelbarrow race, a jumping race, a backward race, a rolling race, or a walking race. Give a prize to everyone who finishes each race. The prize could be a paper ribbon that says, "I have fought the good fight, I have finished the race, I have kept the faith." (See Appendix B for a pattern.)

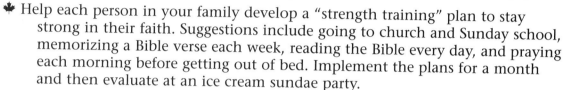

🍁 Have a contest to see who can make the most creative crown of righteousness.

🍁 Attend a local race or sporting event. When it is over, compare it to the faith race for the crown of righteousness. How are they the same? How are they different?

🍁 Help each person in your family develop a "strength training" plan to stay strong in their faith. Suggestions include going to church and Sunday school, memorizing a Bible verse each week, reading the Bible every day, and praying each morning before getting out of bed. Implement the plans for a month and then evaluate at an ice cream sundae party.

🍁 Have each one in your family draw someone's name from a hat and write notes of encouragement to that person. Your notes could say, "Fight the good fight," "With Jesus you can win the race," or "Stand strong in your faith." Think of other words of encouragement. Hide the notes to find over the next few days.

Our Response to God's Grace

Dear Gracious Heavenly Father,

Help us to finish the race so when we stand before You, we may be found faithful and be given the crown of righteousness. For Jesus' sake. Amen.

Ponderings

✍ The apostle Paul, who wrote the letters to Timothy, was flogged, beaten with rods, stoned, shipwrecked, and imprisoned. He labored long and suffered constant hardships. He went hungry and thirsty and often he went without sleep. He was at times cold and naked. For 30 years he faced numerous dangers, often barely escaping death. Now, as he wrote his second epistle to Timothy, he knew his work was done—his life would soon end at the hands of his enemies.

☙ Even as he faced death, his spirit faced life. Paul had fought the good fight. He had persevered. He held strong to faith in Christ until the end. He had won the race and looked forward to his prize—the crown of righteousness, eternal life in heaven.

☙ Paul completed the race and was given the prize, but Paul was not the only one participating in the race. We too are running the race of faith. As we persevere to the end, we too shall be given the crown of righteousness. "Now there is in store for me the crown of righteousness … and not only to me, but also to all who have longed for His appearing" (2 Timothy 4:8b).

☙ Spend some time considering your faith race. Where have you stumbled? What obstacles have you encountered? How has God encouraged and uplifted you? How are you training for the race? Do you come into God's presence in worship and dine at His Table? Do you participate in Bible study?

☙ Paul writes, "For I am already being poured out like a drink offering" (2 Timothy 4:6). Because Christ was poured out as an offering for us, we, like Paul, can offer our lives in loving service to Christ, as He strengthens us to the end and gives us our prize of eternal life.

Journal Jottings

Mapping the Route

God's Grace to Us

Today's Reading: Isaiah 48:17–19

This is what the LORD says—your Redeemer, the Holy One of Israel: "I am the LORD your God, who teaches you what is best for you, who directs you in the way you should go." Isaiah 48:17

Faith Walk

Hike in an unfamiliar place, such as a state park you have never visited or a new trail. When finished, give each family member a piece of paper and some markers. Have each person independently draw a "map" of the area you hiked. Compare the maps. How are they similar? How are they different? Are they accurate?

Faith Talk

✧ Why do we use maps?

✧ How is God's Word like a map?

✧ To what destination does God's Word lead us?

✧ It is important for maps to be accurate or they may lead us to the wrong place. But God's Word is entirely accurate. It clearly lays out for us God's plan for salvation—the way to heaven. It clearly leads us and guides us on our journey through life.

Follow-up Activities

❦ Count all the maps in your home. How many did you find? Did you count the Bibles? How many Bibles do you have?

❧ Hide God's Word, the Bible. Draw a map leading the way from a designated starting point to the Bible. Have your family use the map to find the Bible. What destination does the Bible point to? What does it teach us about getting there?

❧ Find items that represent the treasures we receive from God's Word. For example, a cross can represent forgiveness or a heart pendant can represent God's love. Hide these "treasures" around the house and write clues to help find them. Send your family on a treasure hunt looking for them. What does each treasure stand for? What kinds of treasures do we find in God's Word?

❧ Write a list of the directions God gives us in His map, the Word. Remember that we are not alone in following the map of God's Word. He is with us, teaching us, encouraging us, and helping us. He forgives us and sets us on the right path when we take a wrong turn.

Our Response to God's Grace

Dear Heavenly Father,

Help us to follow your Word each day as You lead us in our walk of faith. We pray in the name of Jesus, who is the Way, the Truth, and the Life. Amen.

Ponderings

🙠 Have you ever attempted to find a new destination without directions or a map? What happened? Were there consequences? Most of us would never consider making a cross-country road trip without a map. Yet many people journey through life each day without the map of God's Word. What happens? Are there consequences to living without God's Word?

🙠 Write some thoughts about the various ways God has led you through His Word. What blessings does He continue to grant to you through His Word and the sacraments of His grace?

🙠 In what ways have you failed to follow? Have you experienced personal consequences?

✎ Read 1 John 1:8–9. In this passage we learn that we all sin. We all fail. Not one of us can follow God's Word perfectly. But we are not without hope. If we confess that we have sinned and have failed to follow God's Word, He will—and does—forgive us. It will be as if we have never failed. This is the greatest treasure to which God leads us in His Word. Praise Him for leading you to His forgiveness!

✎ If you do not already keep a devotional journal, consider starting one to keep a written account of the path on which God is leading you through His Word. If you already keep a devotional journal, review some past entries, consider God's faithfulness and guidance, and praise God for the gift of His Word.

Journal Jottings

Infinity and Beyond

God's Grace to Us

Today's Reading: Jeremiah 23:23–24

"Am I only a God nearby," declares the Lord, "and not a God far away? Can anyone hide in secret places so that I cannot see him?" Jeremiah 23:23–24a

Faith Walk

Hike to the top of a high hill or into the middle of an open field. Gaze into the sky. Think about and discuss the outer boundaries of the universe. Can you even begin to imagine them?

Faith Talk

✧ Think about "bigness." How big is the universe? Is there anything bigger? What does "infinity" mean?

✧ Read the Bible passage. Where is God? How big is God?

✧ Why can the word "infinity" be used to describe God?

✧ How do you feel knowing God is everywhere?

✧ If God is with us all the time, that means He knows about every sin. That's a scary thought. But it need not frighten us because God forgives us. We can take comfort in knowing that wherever we are, our loving God is also. Why is "God Everywhere" a blessing?

Follow-up Activities

❧ Take a trip to your library and check out some books about the solar system. As you look through the books, talk about how God is present throughout *every* solar system.

❦ Gaze into the sky on a starry night. How far can you see? If you have a telescope, use it to study the sky and the stars. As far as your eye can see, as far as a telescope can help you see, beyond the farthest reaches of the universe, God is there.

❦ Tie two-foot lengths of string into loops, one for each family member. Place the loops in circles on the ground outside. Study the space inside the loops. What is the smallest thing you see? Even those small places are not hidden from God. *God is everywhere!*

❦ Read Genesis chapter 3. Adam and Eve tried to hide from God but failed. Can we hide from God when we sin? Is this good or bad? Why?

❦ Play "Hide and Seek." Remember that we can't hide from God's love. Praise be to "God Everywhere!"

Our Response to God's Grace

Dear Father in Heaven,

Just as You fill every place and are not limited to space, so too Your love is everywhere and is without limits! Praise to You whose presence and love go to infinity and beyond! In Jesus' name. Amen.

Ponderings

✐ "You can't put God in a box." So goes the saying. But often people try. They try to crush and contort God to fit a very small place in our lives. Perhaps we think God belongs only in the box of Sunday worship or bedtime prayers. That's where we want Him to stay, but God will not be boxed. In Jeremiah 23:24, our God says, "Do I not fill heaven and earth?" God bursts forth from our boxes and fills everything. In every place and in every moment, God is present! *God is everywhere!*

✐ We can't snap our fingers to make pain disappear, wake up to find our broken relationships restored, or bring peace to a warring world. We are limited, so we put God in a box and try to limit Him too. We say things like, "This problem is too big for even God." Or, "God can't forgive *that* sin." But in

Luke 1:37 we read, "For nothing is impossible with God." Our Almighty God bursts forth from our boxes with limitless power to heal even our largest hurts! *God is everywhere!*

- Perhaps we hear, "God is 'out there,' a being who rules creation from a distance. He doesn't really know me." Such a statement indicates how some try to pack God away into a box in our mental attic, away from a personal relationship. Read Psalm 139. God knows us intimately. He even came to the earth as a man and felt all the joys and sorrows that His beloved children experience. God bursts out of the box and into a personal, loving relationship with us! *God is everywhere!*

- "God was speaking only to the people long ago. Life is different now." Designer religion. Values clarification. Tolerance. Through it all, society stuffs God into a box labeled "man's image." We think we can change God to fit our desires, but Hebrews 13:8 says, "Jesus Christ is the same yesterday and today and forever." God bursts forth from our boxes, a changeless God whose laws are eternal but whose love and promises are also eternal! *God is everywhere!*

- "You can't put God in a box." Our God is big—almighty, all-powerful, all knowing, and with a love that will never change. It is this God, wrapped in the body of a man that burst forth from the grave, who shatters the box in which sin captures us. No one can put God in a box. And because God will not be boxed, we too are free. *God is everywhere!*

Journal Jottings

Food Shelf Servant Event

God's Grace to Us

Today's Reading: Acts 9:36–42

In Joppa there was a disciple named Tabitha (which, when translated, is Dorcas), who was always doing good and helping the poor. Acts 9:36

Faith Walk

Take walks around your neighborhood on two different days. For the first walk, write and deliver letters to your neighbors inviting them to share their food with those less fortunate by placing canned food on their doorstep. Tell them the time and day of your second walk when you will take a wagon around the neighborhood to collect the food, then deliver it a local food shelf or pantry.

Faith Talk

✧ Read through the entire Bible story told in Acts 9:36–42. What blessings can you find as you read the story?

✧ How has God blessed you?

✧ How can you be a blessing to others?

✧ Read verse 42 again. How did God use Tabitha and this event to bring people to faith?

✧ How can our care for others help to draw them into the body of Christ?

Follow-up Activities

❧ Make and deliver notes to your neighbors thanking them for their generosity and telling them how much food was collected. Include a Bible verse such as Proverbs 28:27a.

❦ Ask your pastor about other organizations in the community or church that offer assistance to those in need. As a family, choose one group to support on a regular basis.

❦ Next time you take an out-of-town trip, take some canned goods along as a donation to a local food pantry. This is a wonderful way to share the wealth of your blessings.

❦ Read the daily newspaper with an eye for the needs of others around the world. Pray for them and, when possible, send a check to relief organizations that help in times of crisis.

❦ Start a sock drive at your school or through a local youth organization. Collect and give socks to local homeless shelters.

Our Response to God's Grace

Dear Compassionate Father and Lord,

Help us to reach out to others so they might be blessed with the same love through which You have blessed us. For the sake of Jesus Christ, our Lord. Amen.

Ponderings

❦ "In Joppa there was a disciple named Tabitha. ..." Tabitha was a follower of Christ. She knew Jesus as her Lord and Savior. She was baptized into the faith and was a student of the Gospel. Tabitha had been given a new heart and a changed life.

❦ "... who was always doing good and helping the poor. ..." From the biblical account, it would appear that Tabitha was wealthy. She was financially well off, but her greatest wealth was the abundance of God's love to her. In return, the love of a servant heart flowed from her faith. Her discipleship wasn't merely words, but action. She lived her faith as she reached out to the poor, sharing her wealth and helping them in their need.

❦ "About that time she became sick and died. ... All the widows stood around [Peter], crying and showing him the robes and other clothing [Tabitha] had made. ..." Why? Why Lord? Why must this happen? Our hearts are hurting! The widows cried out in grief and despair.

🖎 "Then [Peter] called the believers and the widows and presented her to them alive. This became known all over Joppa and many people believed in the Lord." Tabitha's fruits of love were fruits of faith. Because Tabitha had been made one with Christ through Baptism, she was a new creation, empowered to offer her heart as a Christ-like servant. As Christ was raised to life to bring life to all believers, Tabitha was raised to life so others might believe and receive life. Christ brings life! Alleluia! Rejoice!

🖎 How can you offer yourself as a living sacrifice and be a servant through which Christ can draw others into the life He alone can bring?

Journal Jottings

Helping Hands Hike

God's Grace to Us

Today's Reading: Ecclesiastes 4:9–12

Though one may be overpowered, two can defend themselves. A cord of three strands is not quickly broken. Ecclesiastes 4:12

Faith Walk

Take a hike in rugged terrain, such as through a densely wooded area or up a mountain trail. Use this opportunity to encourage your family to reach out to one another with helping hands.

Faith Talk

✧ Study the Bible passage. How can two people be stronger together than each one alone?

✧ Three strands are used in a braid. How does the third strand strengthen the cord? Who is the third strand referred to in verse 12?

✧ How can each person in your family build up and support one another?

✧ How can you call on God to be the third strand in your family? In what ways does He strengthen you?

✧ What is some rugged terrain your family is facing at the moment? Illness? Job loss? Difficulty in school or with friends? Ask God to strengthen you and help you support one another. Ask Him to be the strong third cord in your family.

Follow-up Activities

✤ Have each family member use three pieces of yarn to make a braid. Attach the braids to index cards. Write Ecclesiastes 4:12 on each card. Keep the cards by your bed as a reminder that a cord of three strands cannot easily be broken.

✤ Have some fun playing games outside. Do some sporting activities that encourage cooperation, such as building a pyramid, playing softball, or working together to keep a ball up in the air.

✤ Trace someone's hand and cut it out. Stick it on the refrigerator. When you catch a family member lending a helping hand or being an encourager, hand it to him or her with a "thank you!"

✤ Plan a project your family can do together, such as building a tree house or designing a family web site. Divide the tasks and make an effort to encourage one another.

✤ Use wood glue to attach the ends of two ½" × 6" dowels together. Walk around holding only one of the dowels. Do they stay together? Use three dowels to make a triangle. Does it stay together? Just as the triangle is the strongest shape, we are strongest when we are connected as three—God, other Christians, and ourselves. Can you think of ways this is true in life?

Our Response to God's Grace

Dear Father, God of Strength,

Strengthen our family to support one another and claim the strength that can be found only in You. Help us to be a cord of three strands that is not easily broken. In Jesus' strength. Amen.

Ponderings

✐ "A cord of three strands is not quickly broken." In biblical times, cords were used for many tough jobs, including rigging boats, pulling carts, binding prisoners, and making fishnets. Cords needed to be very strong. What are some tough challenges you face that require great strength to overcome?

🕊️ "A cord of three strands is not quickly broken." Reflect on a time in your life when you were at a breaking point or maybe even broken. Did you seek the strength God has to offer? If you keep a journal, explore that time through writing. Compare your written thoughts with those in today's verse.

🕊️ "A cord of three strands is not quickly broken." Three is a number of perfection. God is three, yet one—Father, Son, and Holy Spirit. After three days Christ rose from the grave. Three visitors came to Abraham and announced the fulfillment of God's promise. And a cord of three—a person, a friend, and the Lord—cannot be easily broken. The strength of the three strands enables us to persevere through trials.

🕊️ God holds out a gift to you, the gift of strength from others and, more important, the gift of His unconditional, undying love that will stand by you through all trials.

🕊️ Cling to God and the strength that can be found in Him. Know that His love carries you through all difficulties. Look to the cross. See your bloodied Lord hanging there. He knows your pain. He knows your suffering. He will give you strength.

Journal Jottings

Garbage Collection Day

God's Grace to Us

Today's Reading: Psalm 24

The earth is the LORD's, and everything in it, the world, and all who live in it. Psalm 24:1

Faith Walk

Take along a garbage bag as you walk around your neighborhood. Pick up all the trash you find.

Faith Talk

✧ How should we treat things that belong to others?

✧ According to the Bible passage, to whom does the earth belong? What else belongs to God?

✧ Everything belongs to God. All that we have is a blessing, a gift from Him. He gives us all our blessings out of love for us. In return and out of love for God, how shall we use the gifts with which He has blessed us?

✧ Not only do all things belong to God, but all people also belong to God. God created us. Through Baptism, we are His very own children. What does this mean for our relationship with Him?

✧ Stewardship means to take good care of something that has been given to us or entrusted to our care. We are to be good stewards of God's world and of our lives because everything belongs to God and His blessings are a gift to us from Him. Brainstorm a list of ways to be good stewards of God's blessings.

Follow-up Activities

♣ Give your children three banks—a *spending* bank, a *saving* bank, and a *giving* bank. Every time your children receive or earn some money, have them divide the money between the three banks. This will begin to teach them how to be good stewards of the blessings God has given them.

♣ Touch various body parts and say, as a family, "My _____ belongs to God. It is a gift from Him." Have each person think of ways to use his or her body to glorify God. Examples: "I can glorify God with my ears by listening to wholesome music." "I can glorify God by using my hands to help Mom with the dishes."

♣ How can you be a better steward of your home? Come up with one household project that needs to be done and work on it together as a family.

♣ Write notes to stick around the house that say, "The _____ is God's." Fill in the blanks with household items such as bed, television, computer, etc.

Our Response to God's Grace

Dear God, Gracious Father,

Thank You for the blessings You have given us out of love. Help us to be good stewards of Your gifts and to use them wisely. Everything belongs to You. In Jesus' name. Amen.

Ponderings

✐ Reread Psalm 24:1–2. Do the words found in this verse offer a new perspective or change your thinking in any way? We frequently think *my things, my family, my body—mine, mine, mine*. But in reality nothing is truly ours. Everything belongs to God. This concept can bring radical change to our relationships with things, people, even ourselves. Instead of living our lives based on what is best for us, God helps us to live our lives in accordance with His will as creator and owner of everything.

- Read verses 7–10. These verses offer a picture of God as the King of Glory, the Lord strong and mighty, the Lord mighty in battle—the Lord Almighty. He is our powerful, glorious Ruler!

- God is indeed our Ruler, our King; we are His subjects. Meditate on the following phrases from Psalm 24 that offer insight into what it means to give honor to God, our King:

  He who has clean hands
  A pure heart
  Does not lift up his soul to an idol or swear by what is false
      (all from verse 4)
  Seek Him (verse 6)
  Lift up your heads, O you gates; be lifted up you ancient doors (verse 9)

- Read Galatians 3:26–4:7. As subjects of God, we are blessed, for He has made us not only His subjects, but also His heirs through Christ Jesus. We are children of God!

- Read again Psalm 24:5–6. God pours His blessings out upon those who trust in Him, His subjects and His heirs!

Journal Jottings

Appendix A

Tips for Building a Spiritually Uplifting Family Devotional Life

Hear, O Israel: The LORD our God, the LORD is one. Love the LORD your God with all your heart and with all your soul and with all your strength. These commandments that I give you today are to be upon your hearts. Impress them on your children. Talk about them when you sit at home and when you walk along the road, when you lie down, and when you get up. Tie them as symbols on your hands and bind them on your foreheads. Write them on the doorframes of your houses and on your gates. Deuteronomy 6:4–9

Walking with God All Day, Every Day

In Matthew 28:20, Jesus gives us an awesome promise when He says, "And surely I am with you always, to the very end of the age." God—Father, Son, and Holy Spirit—is with us always, reaching out to us in love, and walking with us through each day.

In the above verses from Deuteronomy, God holds out to us both an invitation and a command. He invites and commands us to love Him with our whole being as He has loved us. It is easy to relegate God to only portions of our lives, but He wants to encompass all of our family life. He is with us when we are asleep and when we are awake, when we are home and when we are away from home. Our loving Lord desires that throughout each day we remind our children that they are His own, baptized and redeemed. He desires that we bring our children to His house in worship and that in our own homes we point them to His love. In so doing, we also teach them how to love Him in return. This is the key to not only a spiritually uplifting family devotional life, but also to lives of devotion that flow from God back to God.

Faith Communication

Talk with your children about God and His love. Teach them about their faith in Christ:

✧ Make a Baptism banner for each child and hang it in a prominent place.

✧ Tell your children the stories of God's faithfulness throughout the Old Testament and His promise to send a Savior.

✧ Tell them the stories of Jesus—the Savior who was the fulfillment of that promise.

✧ Teach your children about God's forgiveness through Christ. Forgive them when they do wrong and teach them how to forgive one another.

✧ Remind your children how God would have us live as His own children.

✧ Tell your own faith stories about how God has touched your life.

✧ Let your children ask questions, even the hard questions.

✧ Ask them challenging questions such as, "Why do you think there is pain in the world?" and "How do we know that the Christian faith is the one true faith?" Encourage your children, with help, to struggle to find the answers so their faith becomes more personal.

✧ Seek the answers to their questions and your own. Talk to your pastor, study God's Word, attend Bible studies, arm yourself with faith-teaching resources such as *Luther's Small Catechism* or Bible commentaries.

✧ Make faith communication a part of every day. Share your faith when you drive to ball practice, when you greet your child after school, when you eat a meal together, and when you say good morning or kiss your young ones good night.

Powerful Prayer

"And pray in the Spirit on all occasions with all kinds of prayers and requests" (Ephesians 6:18a).

God has provided a wonderful opportunity for us as He invites us to pray. One indicator of a Christian family strong in faith is that they come to God through prayer in times of both difficulty and joy.

The following acronyms are often given as models for prayer. They will help guide you and your family into a well-rounded and meaningful prayer life.

PRAY

P—Praise: Give praises to God.

R—Repent: Confess your sins and ask for God's forgiveness through Jesus.

A—Ask: Ask God to provide for both spiritual and material needs for yourselves and others.

Y—Yield: Put your prayers and requests into God's hands saying, "Let Your will be done."

ACTS

A—Adoration: Lift up your praises to God.

C—Confession: Confess your sins and seek forgiveness.

T—Thanksgiving: Thank the Lord for the many blessings He has rained down upon you.

S—Supplications: Ask God to supply your needs and those of others.

In addition to these prayer models, there are many other ways to make prayer a rich part of your family's spiritual heritage. Here are additional ideas:

✧ **Stop, drop, and pray.** God tells us in 1 Thessalonians 5:16 to "pray continually." One way to model this for children is to pray at various times throughout each day. Pray a prayer of praise when it rains after a long dry spell, ask for God's healing when a child gets hurt, or lift up a prayer of thanksgiving when an unexpected check arrives during a financially tight time.

✧ **Share God's answers to prayers.** Teach your children that God answers all prayer—but sometimes not in the manner we expect. God might answer with a "yes," "no," or "wait." Whatever the answer, we can be certain God answers our prayers for our good. When you see an answer to a prayer, talk about it with your children so they can see firsthand the power that God works through prayer.

✧ **Set aside regular times for prayer.** In the morning, before meals, during devotions, and before going to bed are all excellent times to spend a quiet moment talking with God.

✧ **Learn memorized prayers.** The Lord's Prayer, mealtime prayers, psalms, and other memorized prayers teach us about prayer and give us insight for enriching our prayer lives.

✧ **Keep a family prayer journal.** Use a journal to record your praises, your petitions, and your thanksgiving. Occasionally reread to review how God has been faithful, strengthening your family and your life through His answers to prayer.

✧ **Pray playfully.** Just as children often laugh and have fun with their parents, having fun coming to their heavenly Father in prayer can teach them that their faith is joyful. Try these ideas for adding versatility and joy to your family prayers:

1. Pass a beanbag around a circle while taking turns praying.

2. Draw pictures of your prayers.

3. Sing prayer songs.

4. Wad up a sheet of newspaper for each sin you confess in prayer. Stuff the "sins" into a garbage bag and throw them away as a reminder that Christ has "thrown away" our sins.

5. Develop other playful ideas for adding joy to your prayers!

Daily Prayers

The following suggestions are from Martin Luther, a father of seven. He offers these as models for the head of the household to follow in leading the family in prayer. While written in the 16th century, they can still be applied today.

Morning Prayer

In the morning when you get up, make the sign of the holy cross and say:

In the name of the Father and of the Son and of the Holy Spirit. Amen.

Then, kneeling or standing, repeat the Creed and the Lord's Prayer. If you choose, you may also say this little prayer:

I thank You, my heavenly Father, through Jesus Christ, Your dear Son, that You have kept me this day from all harm and danger; and I pray that You would keep me this day also from sin and every evil, that all my doings and life may please You. For into Your hands I commend myself, my body and soul, and all things. Let your holy angel be with me, that the wicked foe may have no power over me. Amen.

Then go joyfully to your work, singing a hymn, like that of the Ten Commandments, or whatever your devotion may suggest.

Evening Prayer

In the evening when you go to bed, make the sign of the holy cross and say:

In the name of the Father and of the Son and of the Holy Spirit. Amen.

Then kneeling or standing, repeat the Creed and the Lord's Prayer. If you choose, you may also say this little prayer:

I thank You, my heavenly Father, through Jesus Christ, Your dear Son, that You have graciously kept me this day; and I pray that You would forgive me all my sins where I have done wrong, and graciously keep me this night. For into your hands I commend myself, my body and soul and all things. Let Your holy angel be with me, that the evil foe may have no power over me. Amen.

Then go sleep at once and in good cheer.

Asking a Blessing

The children and members of the household shall go to the table reverently, fold their hands, and say:

The eyes of all look to You, [O Lord] and You give them their food at the proper time. You open Your hand and satisfy the desires of every living thing (Psalm 145:15–16).

Then shall be said the Lord's Prayer and the following:

Lord God, heavenly Father, bless us and these Your gifts which we receive from Your bountiful goodness, through Jesus Christ, our Lord. Amen.

Returning Thanks

Also, after eating, they shall, in like manner, reverently and with folded hands say:

Give thanks to the Lord, for He is good. His love endures forever. [He] gives food to every creature. He provides food for the cattle and for the young ravens when they call. His pleasure is not in the strength of the horse, nor His delight in the legs of a man; the Lord delights in those who fear Him, who put their hope in His unfailing love (Psalm 136:1, 25; 147:9–11).

Then shall be said the Lord's Prayer and the following:

We thank You, Lord God, heavenly Father, for all Your benefits, through Jesus Christ, our Lord, who lives and reigns with You and the Holy Spirit forever and ever. Amen.

Digging into God's Word

In Deuteronomy, God implores parents to impress His Words on the hearts of their children. This is best done when families make it a practice to study God's Word. Here are some tips to help you make God's Word a part of your family heart:

✧ **Read the Bible daily**. Consider purchasing a children's study Bible to help your children read and understand God's Word. One such resource is the *Faith Alive Bible* (Concordia Publishing House, 1995). Grade-school age children are usually eager to read God's Word, making this a perfect time to develop a family habit of Bible study.

✧ **Make use of Bible study resources**.

1. Are you trying to remember who Absalom was or wanting to teach your child about real joy? Look up the words in a Bible concordance, often found in the back of a study Bible, and find Bible passages that answer your questions.

2. Maps of lands in Bible times can help your family better understand the history that surrounds a Bible story.

3. Many study Bibles have notes that open up the meaning of a Bible passage for readers.

✧ **Become a scientist—dissect Bible passages.**

1. Discuss the meaning of a particular verse. Be sure to read the verses around it to help put it into context.

2. Look up other passages that relate to what you are reading. Use text notes or a concordance to find related passages.

3. As you read the Bible, take notes in the form of questions and answers. Use them later for a homemade Bible trivia game.

✧ **Impress God's Words upon your hearts by memorizing them.** In so doing, God's Word becomes a part of you and your children, carrying you through each day. Try these fun ideas to help:

1. Start with the first word of a Bible verse and go around in a circle, having each family member take a turn saying the word that follows.

2. Illustrate a Bible passage.

3. Set the words to music. Use a familiar tune or make up a silly ditty.

4. Write the words on paper, then cut the paper into pieces to turn the Bible verse into a puzzle.

5. Create actions to go with a particular Bible verse.

6. Use a Bible passage as a cheer.

Worship Wiggle Wompers

"Is it over yet?" If you've heard these words more than once in church, it might be time to try a few tactics for making the worship experience more meaningful for your children:

✧ **Extend worship into the week.**

1. During the week, practice singing songs and praying prayers that are commonly used in your church so your children can better participate on Sunday morning.

2. If possible, find out before the service what the Scripture readings, theme of the day, and focus of the sermon will be, then discuss them with your children so they can better understand the service on Sunday.

3. Review church etiquette. Take time during the week to discuss, in positive terms, the proper behavior in church and why.

✧ **Smooth out Sunday morning wrinkles—and not just in church clothes.**

1. Get your children to bed early on Saturday night.

2. Lay out church clothes the night before.

3. Pray for God's presence with you in worship the next morning.

4. Speak with enthusiasm and joy about going to church the next day.

✧ **Involve your child in the service**.

1. Have your children bring their own offering to church.

2. Teach even the youngest child to fold her hands during prayers.

3. Bring quiet activities for little children, but choose items with a spiritual focus, such as a children's Bible or a Bible character coloring book.

4. Have older children take notes on the sermon or keep a tally of how many times a key word, such as "Jesus," was said during the sermon or the service.

5. Encourage your children to listen by reviewing the service at home later.

Potpourri of Ideas

The best gift we can give our children is to help them see God's love everywhere. Here are some additional ideas for helping you weave God into every part of your days:

✧ **Make mealtimes meaningful.**

　1. Vary the prayers to include memorized and made-up prayers.

　2. Ask a question-of-the-day at supper to generate a discussion about faith. Here are a few ideas to get you started: "How do we get to heaven?" "How can we witness our faith to our friends?" "Why is lying wrong?"

　3. Light candles and read from Scripture before eating.

　4. Use mealtimes as an opportunity to listen to your children and learn where their hearts are.

✧ **Look for God in ordinary things.**

　1. A key can be a reminder that Jesus is the "key" to heaven.

　2. When we look at a chair, we can be reminded that we shouldn't be only sitting around but be out and about, sharing God's love.

　3. A toy soldier can remind us to pray for the military.

　4. How can you help your children see God in ordinary objects?

✧ **Turn on a Christian radio station or play Christian CDs.**

✧ **Use visual faith reminders in your home.** A picture of Jesus, a cross in a curio cabinet, Christian window clings, and a Christ-centered sun catcher all reflect your faith and teach your children that faith seeps into every area of life.

✧ **Be a literature missionary.** Encourage your children to read Christian literature. Several exciting Christian book series are available for school-aged youth. And remember to read Christian literature yourself.

✧ **Build a foundation of forgiveness.** The heart of the Christian faith is Christ crucified and the forgiveness He offers. Practice repentance and forgiveness, and daily remind your children of the forgiveness they receive through Jesus.

Appendix B

Projects and Patterns

Play Dough Recipe

Ingredients

   2 c. flour
   1 c. salt
   4 tsp. cream of tarter
   1 pkg. unsweetened powdered fruit drink mix
   2 c. water
   4 T. vegetable oil

Directions

   Combine flour, salt, cream of tarter, and fruit drink mix in a large saucepan. Combine water and oil separately in a bowl. Gradually add liquid to dry ingredients. Cook over medium heat, stirring constantly, until mixture forms a ball. Remove from heat. Allow play dough to cool until you can comfortably handle it. Knead until smooth. Store in an airtight container or zipper bag.

Clay Heart Ornaments

Materials

1 c. salt
1 c. flour
1 T. alum
Water (enough to make
  dough workable consistency)

Heart-shaped cookie cutter
Red paint
Dull pencil
Ribbon

Directions

Mix salt, flour, and alum. Add water until the mixture is the consistency of putty. Roll out dough to ¼–½" thickness. Cut out hearts with heart-shaped cookie cutter. Poke a hole in the hearts with dull pencil. Allow to dry. Paint with red paint. String a ribbon through the hole and tie a loop.

Note: Ornaments may be made ahead of time. Children can then paint them and string the ribbon through the hole. Or this project may be completed on two separate occasions.

Crystal Garden

Materials

Pie tin
Charcoal
½ c. water
½ c. salt

½ c. liquid bluing
1 c. ammonia
Green, yellow, and blue food coloring

Directions

Cover the bottom of the pie tin with charcoal. Mix water, salt, liquid bluing, and ammonia. Pour mixture over charcoal so all of the charcoal is saturated. Squirt a few drops of food coloring over charcoal (avoid red). Let set overnight. Voila! A crystal garden!

Patterns

Heart Pattern (See pages 26 and 112.)

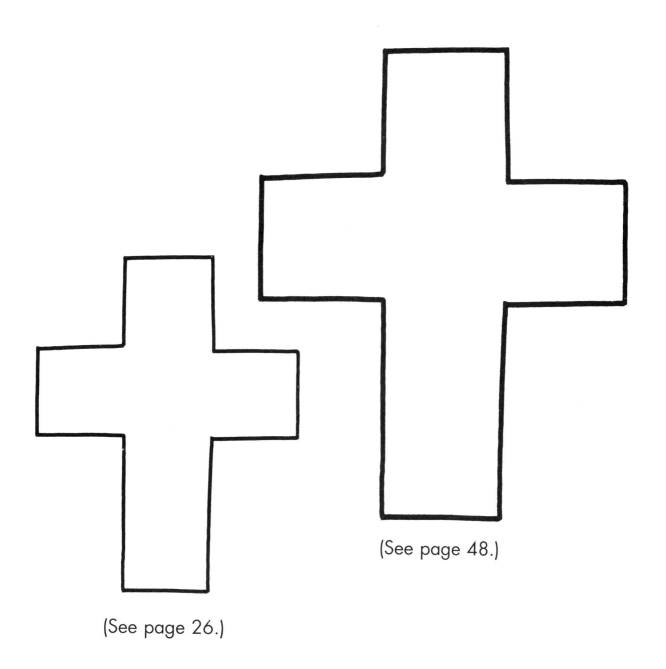

(See page 48.)

(See page 26.)

Cross Pattern

Lamb Pattern (See page 39.)

Three-leaf-clover Pattern (See page 58.)

Palm Branch Pattern (See page 70.)

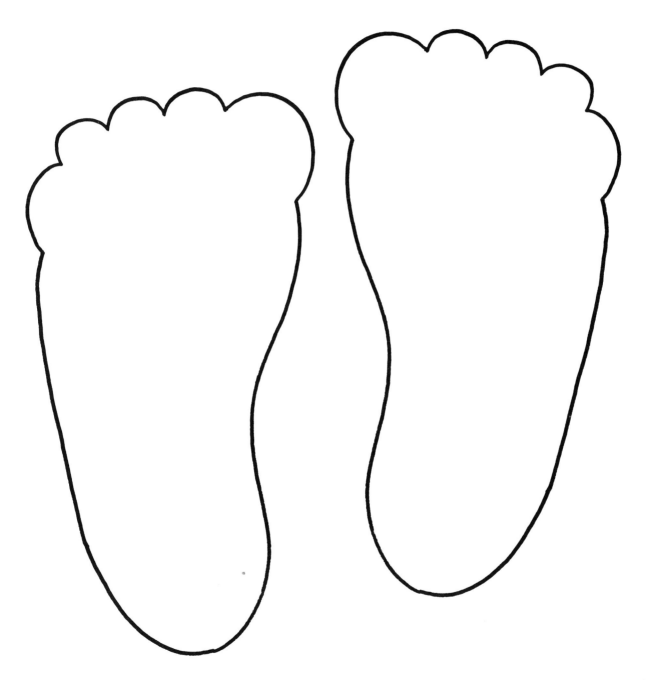

Footprint Pattern (See page 83.)

Dove Pattern (See page 105.)

Family Shield Pattern (See page 129.)

Star Pattern (See page 136.)

Bible Pattern (See page 180. Enlarge as necessary.)

Fruit Patterns (See page 180.)

Fruit Patterns (See page 180.)

Buckle of Truth Pattern (See page 196.)

Breastplate of Righteousness Pattern (See page 196.)

Shield of Faith Pattern (See page 196.)

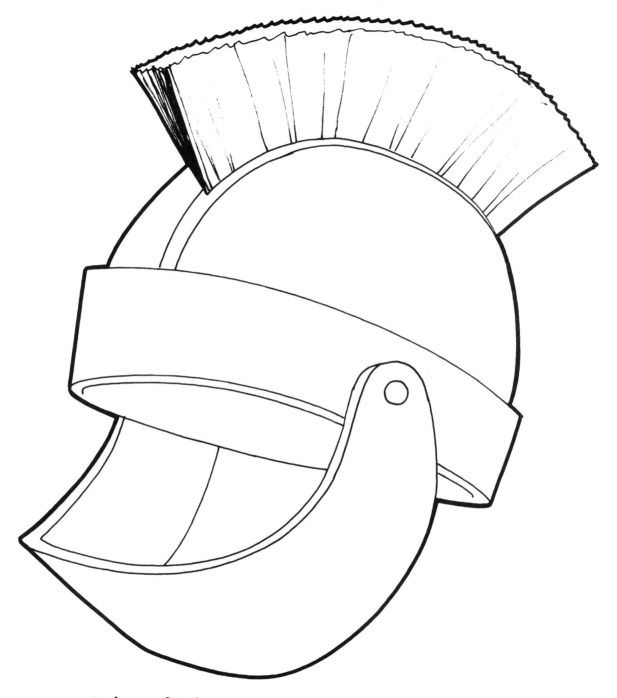

Helmet of Salvation Pattern (See page 196.)

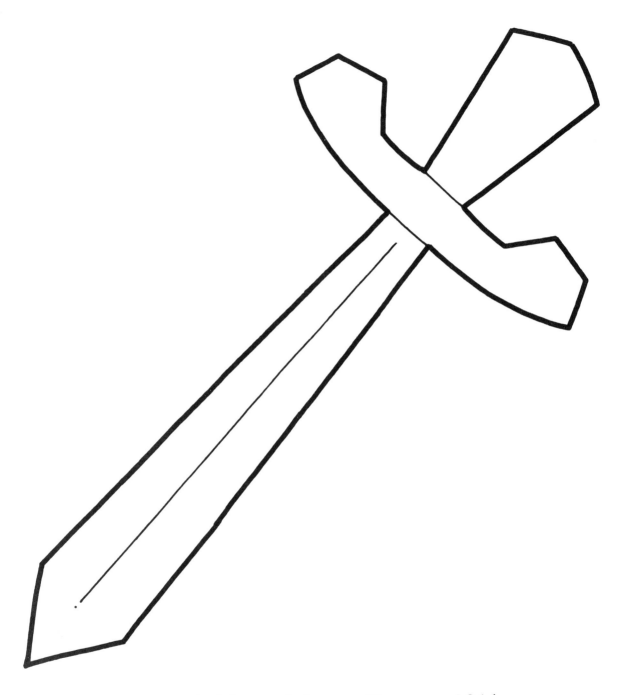

Sword of the Spirit Pattern (See page 196.)

Ten Commandments Tablet Pattern (See page 252.)

Ribbon Pattern (See pages 254–255.)